D0622905

DISEASES AND DISORDERS

THE DANGERS OF **SEXUALLY TRANSMITTED DISEASES**

By Christine Honders

Portions of this book originally appeared in *Sexually Transmitted Diseases* by Terri Dougherty.

WITHDRAWN

LUCENT PRESS

Published in 2018 by
Lucent Press, an Imprint of Greenhaven Publishing LLC
353 3rd Avenue
Suite 255
New York, NY 10010

Copyright © 2018 Greenhaven Press, a part of Gale, Cengage Learning
Gale and Greenhaven Press are registered trademarks used herein under license.

All new materials copyright © 2018 Lucent Press, an Imprint of Greenhaven Publishing LLC.

All rights reserved. No part of this book may be reproduced in any form without permission in writing from the publisher, except by a reviewer.

Designer: Andrea Davison-Bartolotta
Editor: Vanessa Oswald

Cataloging-in-Publication Data

Names: Honders, Christine.
Title: The dangers of sexually transmitted diseases / Christine Honders.
Description: New York : Lucent Press, 2018. | Series: Diseases and disorders | Includes index.
Identifiers: ISBN 9781534561250 (library bound) | ISBN 9781534561267 (ebook)
Subjects: LCSH: Sexually transmitted diseases–Juvenile literature.
Classification: LCC RC200.25 D68 2018 | DDC 616.95'1–dc23

Printed in the United States of America

CPSIA compliance information: Batch #BS17KL: For further information contact Greenhaven Publishing LLC, New York, New York at 1-844-317-7404.

Please visit our website, www.greenhavenpublishing.com. For a free color catalog of all our high-quality books, call toll free 1-844-317-7404 or fax 1-844-317-7405.

CONTENTS

Illness is an unfortunate part of life, and it is one that is often misunderstood. Thanks to advances in science and technology, people have been aware for many years that diseases such as the flu, pneumonia, and chicken pox are caused by viruses and bacteria. These diseases all cause physical symptoms that people can see and understand, and many people have dealt with these diseases themselves. However, sometimes diseases that were previously unknown in most of the world turn into epidemics and spread across the globe. Without an awareness of the method by which these diseases are spread—through the air, through human waste or fluids, through sexual contact, or by some other method—people cannot take the proper precautions to prevent further contamination. Panic often accompanies epidemics as a result of this lack of knowledge.

Knowledge is power in the case of mental disorders, as well. Mental disorders are just as common as physical disorders, but due to a lack of awareness among the general public, they are often stigmatized. Scientists have studied them for years and have found that they are generally caused by hormonal imbalances in the brain, but they have not yet determined with certainty what causes those imbalances or how to fix them. Because even mild mental illness is stigmatized in Western society, many people prefer not to talk about it.

Chronic pain disorders are also not well understood—even by researchers—and do not yet have foolproof treatments. People who have a mental disorder or a disease or disorder that causes them to feel chronic pain can be the target of uninformed opinions. People who do not have these disorders sometimes struggle to understand how difficult it can be to deal with the symptoms. These disorders are often termed "invisible illnesses" because no one can see the symptoms; this leads many people to doubt that they exist or are serious problems. Additionally, people who have an undiagnosed disorder may understand that they are experiencing the world in a different way than their peers, but they have no one to turn to for answers.

Misinformation about all kinds of ailments is often spread through personal anecdotes, social media, and even news sources. This series aims to present accurate information about both physical and mental conditions so young adults will have a better understanding of them. Each volume discusses the symptoms of a particular disease or disorder, ways it is currently being treated, and the research that is being done to understand it further. Advice for people who may be suffering from a disorder is included, as well as information for their loved ones about how best to support them.

With fully cited quotes, a list of recommended books and websites for further research, and informational charts, this series provides young adults with a factual introduction to common illnesses. By learning more about these ailments, they will be better able to prevent the spread of contagious diseases, show compassion to people who are dealing with invisible illnesses, and take charge of their own health.

INTRODUCTION

IT CAN HAPPEN TO ANYONE

Amber was 17 years old. After being with her boyfriend Sean for a long time, they decided to have sex. They felt that they were ready and discussed the possibility of pregnancy, but Amber was on birth control pills, so they were not worried. What they never discussed was the possibility of a sexually transmitted disease (STD). A few days after, Amber noticed small, painless sores on her body. She and Sean decided to get tested, and both found out they had syphilis, which is an STD.

STDs are a serious health problem that impacts everyone. They affect people of all backgrounds, races, ages, and genders. Some STDs, if not treated, can cause lifelong damage. Others cannot be cured.

According to the Centers for Disease Control and Prevention (CDC), every year in the United States, there are 20 million new cases of STDs, and half of those are in young people between the ages of 15 and 24. However, anyone who is sexually active is at risk. A person does not even have to have sex to get an STD; some can be spread by skin-to-skin contact.

Sexually transmitted diseases, also called sexually transmitted infections (STIs), are diseases that can be passed from one person to another through vaginal, oral, or anal sex. Some are easily cured; others are incurable but may be managed with medication for many years. Common STDs include chlamydia; gonorrhea; herpes; the human immunodeficiency virus (HIV), which causes acquired immunodeficiency syndrome (AIDS); and the human papillomavirus (HPV), which causes cervical cancer and genital warts. Syphilis, the oldest known STD, also continues to spread.

STDs Overseas

Until the 1990s, STDs were known as venereal diseases. This name derives from Venus, the Roman goddess of love. Two of the first diseases to be known as venereal diseases were syphilis and gonorrhea. These were the most common STDs in Europe hundreds of years ago. Some believe that Christopher Columbus and his crew brought syphilis to Europe from the Americas. Sailors were also blamed for spreading gonorrhea from Tahiti to New Zealand. Today, more than 20 diseases are classified as STDs.

A Serious Thing

Although STDs are a threat, many teens, such as Amber, do not think they are at risk of infection. However, anyone who has sex can become infected. Susan Cohen has worked in sexuality education for more than 20 years, and she knows how difficult it is for teens to understand that a sexual encounter may have lifelong consequences. "When you're seventeen or eighteen and carefree, you're caught up in what's going on in front of you and it's difficult to see how those decisions you make today, tonight, and tomorrow can affect you years down the line," she said. "But what you do today can affect you tomorrow."[1]

Amber said, "The worst part was asking my parents to make the doctor's appointment. I didn't want them to know I'd had sex ... Luckily they realized what was important was getting me to see a doctor."[2] Getting an STD is embarrassing, but ignoring the symptoms can be life-threatening. Untreated syphilis can cause crippling of the body, mental illness, and deformities in unborn babies of women with the disease.

Amber and Sean were treated with a simple penicillin shot. Amber said, "I know what to look out for now, and how to stay safe and healthy. Even though it was really scary to have the disease, I'm glad I realized how serious things like that can be."[3]

> Half of sexually active young people will get an STD before they turn 25, and many will have no idea.

Everyone's Problem

Learning more about STDs can help people make the right choices regarding sexual activity. It can also inform them about how to minimize their risk of getting an STD or giving an STD to another person. "For the most part, people just don't realize how many people have an STD," said Stuart Berman of the CDC's STD branch. "It's not a rare event. It's part of being a sexually active person. It's not an issue of it being the nasty kid down the block. The bottom line is, it's very common. It's not somebody else's problem."[4]

CHAPTER ONE

A WORSENING EPIDEMIC

Jenelle Marie Pierce is the founder and Executive Director of The STD Project. Started in 2012, The STD Project is an independent website that promotes sexual health by providing resources for education and prevention. Pierce has had three STDs in her life: genital herpes, HPV, and scabies. She encourages others to tell their stories on her website in an effort to promote awareness. Pierce wrote she is still not certain which partner gave her herpes: "I had more than one sexual partner and was too embarrassed/distraught to advocate for myself or ask questions."[5] This website is Pierce's effort toward making sure other people are not afraid to come forward and get treatment.

Pierce has a reason to be concerned. According to a 2015 report by the CDC, the rate of STDs is steadily increasing. That year was the second year in a row where there were increases in all three nationally reported STDs (chlamydia, syphilis, and gonorrhea). Young people and gay men are at the highest risk for infection by far; however, women face more serious, long-term health effects. Congenital syphilis (which occurs when the infection is spread from mother to unborn child) has increased 6 percent since 2014. STD cases cost the United States health care system nearly $16 billion per year. "The resurgence of congenital syphilis and the increasing impact of syphilis among gay and bisexual men makes it clear that many Americans are not getting the preventive services they need,"[6] said Dr. Gail Bolan, who is the director of the CDC's STD prevention division.

The Centers for Disease Control and Prevention (CDC) is the leading national public health institute of the United States. The CDC keeps records on how many people in this country contract STDs each year.

Alarming Rates

Many attempts have been made to stop the spread of STDs, yet these infections remain a major health concern in the United States. The most commonly reported bacterial infection in the United States is chlamydia. According to the CDC, 1.5 million cases of chlamydia were reported in 2015, which was the highest number of cases of any condition ever reported to the agency. In 2007, the rate of people with chlamydia was 370.2 cases per 100,000, and in 2015 it increased to 479 cases per 100,000. The rate has increased around 6 percent in the past two years.

Although the number of reported cases is large, the number of people actually living with chlamydia is even larger. The CDC estimates that less than half of the cases are diagnosed, which means that approximately 3 million people are infected in the United States each year.

The number of reported cases of syphilis and gonorrhea are increasing as well. In 2015, syphilis rates increased 19 percent since the previous year, with almost 24,000 cases reported, and gonorrhea rates increased 13 percent, with more than 395,000 cases reported.

The rate of gonorrhea fell 74 percent from the 1970s to mid-1990s, but that changed in the 2000s, with the national rate increasing slightly each year until 2009, when the rate reached a historic low of 98.1 cases per 100,000. By 2015, the rate had increased to 124 cases per 100,000.

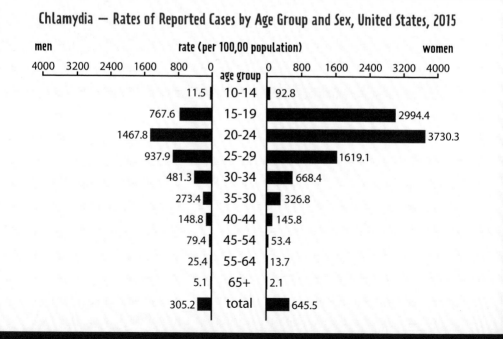

Chlamydia — Rates of Reported Cases by Age Group and Sex, United States, 2015

men						age group	women					
rate (per 100,00 population)												
4000	3200	2400	1600	800	0		0	800	1600	2400	3200	4000
					11.5	10-14	92.8					
				767.6		15-19						2994.4
			1467.8			20-24						3730.3
			937.9			25-29			1619.1			
				481.3		30-34		668.4				
				273.4		35-30		326.8				
				148.8		40-44		145.8				
				79.4		45-54	53.4					
				25.4		55-64	13.7					
				5.1		65+	2.1					
				305.2		total		645.5				

This chart from the CDC shows the breakdown of reported chlamydia cases by age and gender in 2015.

The Tinder Effect

The increased cases of gonorrhea and syphilis are particularly frustrating to public health officials. Between 1975 and 1996, the number of cases of gonorrhea fell by 74 percent. This was largely due to a gonorrhea-control program that was implemented in the mid-1970s. Syphilis, an STD that has been documented for centuries, hit an all-time low in 2000. What happened to cause such a dramatic increase?

Dr. Jonathan Mermin, the director of the National Center for HIV/AIDS, Viral Hepatitis, STD, and TB Prevention, has a few theories. Since the country's economic downturn, in approximately 2009 to 2010, the budgets have been slashed for more than half of the state and local programs that provide testing as well as treatment for STDs. According to Mermin, "Those are among the primary places where we actually diagnose and treat S.T.D.s as well as H.I.V."[1] Dr. Gail Bolan, director of the CDC's Division of STD Prevention, expressed the same concerns: "About 7 percent of health departments have closed STD clinics ... Over 40 percent have reduced clinic hours, and clinics have increased fees and co-pays. We are concerned that people are not getting access to the STD health services they deserve and need."[2]

Many health care officials also blame what they call the Tinder effect, believing that dating websites that promote casual sex encourage people to practice other risky behaviors such as not using birth control. Mermin said that while some local health departments believe there is a connection, at this point, it is not completely clear if there is a cause and effect relationship.

1. Quoted in Abby Goodnough, "Reported Cases of STDs Are on Rise," *New York Times*, October 19, 2016. www.nytimes.com/2016/10/20/us/reported-cases-of-sexually-transmitted-diseases-are-on-rise.html?_r=1.

2. Quoted in Steven Reinberg, "Syphilis, Gonorrhea, Chlamydia Rates Rising for First Time in Years: CDC," HealthDay, November 17, 2015. consumer.healthday.com/sexual-health-information-32/misc-sexually-tranmitted-diseases-news-609/syphilis-gonorrhea-chlamydia-rates-rising-for-first-time-in-years-cdc-705360.html.

Human Papillomavirus (HPV)

HPV is the most common STD—so common that most adults have been infected by it at some point in their lives. In most cases, it goes away on its own and does not cause any health problems. If it does not go away, it can cause problems such as genital warts or cancer.

In 2006, the HPV vaccine was approved for use to stop the health problems some HPV infections can cause. The CDC recommends two doses of the vaccine for all 11- to 12-year-olds to protect against cancers caused by the infection. Since cancer takes years to develop after HPV infection, women between the ages of 21 to 65 should be screened routinely for cervical cancer.

Genital Herpes

Genital herpes is another common STD. Although cases of this disease do not have to be reported to public health officials, it is estimated that in the United States, 1 in 6 people aged 14 to 49 years have genital herpes, which can bring on painful sores. It is caused by the herpes simplex virus type 1 (HSV-1) or type 2 (HSV-2). Herpes is incurable but generally manageable with medications. However, pregnant women can have more complications, including premature labor and miscarriage (when the baby dies in the womb during the first 20 weeks of pregnancy). They can also pass the disease onto the newborn baby and cause a potentially deadly infection called neonatal herpes.

Human Immunodeficiency Virus (HIV)

HIV attacks the body's immune system, specifically T-cells, which are responsible for helping the body fight off infections. Untreated HIV will destroy these T-cells, putting the person at risk for other infections and diseases. Over time, if the T-cells fall below 200 cells per cubic millimeter of blood, the infected person has progressed to AIDS (acquired immunodeficiency syndrome). This stage is when the body is so badly damaged that it becomes vulnerable to other infections. Without treatment, people diagnosed with AIDS have about three years to live.

HIV is incurable and 20 years ago was a death sentence, but the development of new drug therapy has

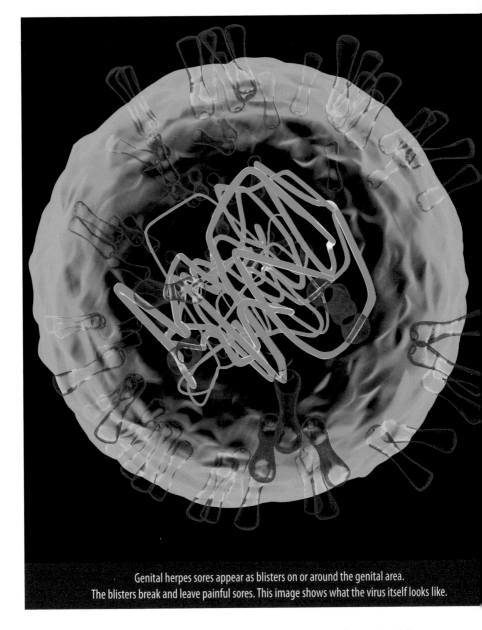

Genital herpes sores appear as blisters on or around the genital area.
The blisters break and leave painful sores. This image shows what the virus itself looks like.

now allowed someone with HIV to live a long, healthy life—even as long as someone without HIV.

Adolescents: At High Risk

Though STDs can affect anyone who is sexually active, they are especially prevalent among young people. According to the CDC, young people aged 15 to 24 account for almost half of all new STD cases each year.

In 2015, 41 percent of high school students reported to have had sexual intercourse, and 30 percent of high school students reported that they had been sexually active within the past three months. About 3.9 percent said they first had sex by the age of 13.

The risks of early sexual contact include STDs. "Sex is an emotional decision, a serious decision, and this is another reason to be serious about that decision," comments Stuart Berman, senior advisor of the CDC's National Center for HIV/AIDS, Viral Hepatitis, STD, and TB Prevention (NCHHSTP) branch. He added that teens need to understand how common and prevalent these infections are, and they need to realize that pregnancy is not the only risk of being sexually active. "It means that sex must not be taken trivially," he said. "It's an important decision. Pregnancy is an important concern, but people also need to be thinking that every time you have sex there's that risk of STDs."[7]

Certain STDs are especially common among young people. Out of all the chlamydia cases in 2015, 66 percent were reported by people between 15 and 24 years old. "I see mostly chlamydia cases," said Suzanne Swanson, a pediatric gynecologist with ThedaCare in Appleton, Wisconsin, "and the problem with chlamydia is it spreads like wildfire."[8]

Health Inequity

Another concern is the difference in STD rates among minority races. In 2015, the rate of chlamydia among blacks was almost 7 times higher than that of whites, and the gonorrhea rate was almost 10 times higher. The rate of chlamydia and gonorrhea among Latinx was around two times higher than whites.

Minority groups are more likely to get STDs for many reasons. The poverty rate for blacks and Latinx is over twice that of whites, and the CDC notes that people who struggle financially are more likely to have a lifestyle that increases their risk for an STD. Additionally, many minority groups distrust the health care system, fearing provider bias, which keeps them from getting tested. Many do not have adequate health care. Also, living in a poverty stricken area where the STD rates are higher increases the odds of a sexually active person becoming infected.

STDs are a problem that must be taken seriously by young people.

Differences in Women

STDs also hit women especially hard. The rate of syphilis diagnoses among women increased by more than 27 percent between 2014 and 2015. By age 50, about 80 percent of women will have contracted an HPV infection at some point in their lives.

HPV can cause genital warts as well as cancer that forms in the cervix, which is the lower part of a woman's uterus. In 2013, more than 4,000 women died from cervical cancer, and more than 11,000 new cases are diagnosed each year, according to the CDC. "Having unprotected sex, especially at a young age, makes HPV infection more likely," the American Cancer Society notes. "Also, women who have many sex partners (or who have sex with men who have had many partners) have a greater chance of getting HPV."[9]

Having an STD can also make it difficult for a person to have children. STDs are the main preventable cause of infertility, according to the CDC. Up to 15 percent of women with gonorrhea and chlamydia will develop pelvic inflammatory disease (PID), which can damage reproductive organs. In 2013, there were 88,000 women between the ages of 15 and 44 diagnosed with PID. The disease causes an infection in a woman's uterus, fallopian tubes, or ovaries. The infection can be treated successfully, but it can cause the fallopian tubes to become scarred. Tubal scarring can cause infertility in 8 percent of women with a history of PID, ectopic (tubal) pregnancy in 9 percent of women, and chronic pain for 18 percent.

Issues also arise when a pregnant woman is infected with an STD. A pregnant woman who has an STD, such as gonorrhea, chlamydia, herpes simplex, or HIV, can pass the infection on to her baby while the child is still in the womb, during childbirth, or immediately after the baby is born. A woman who does not get

Most problems with STDs during pregnancy can be prevented with early testing and treatment.

treated puts her baby at risk for complications. The child may be blind, develop infections, or die shortly after birth. A woman may give birth to a stillborn child (a baby born without any signs of life), and she may be at higher risk for a miscarriage or delivering a premature baby.

STDs and the LGBTQ Community

The rise of STDs among gay and bisexual men is a major concern. In fact, men who have sex with men (MSM) make up the majority of new cases of gonorrhea and syphilis—nearly 82 percent. CDC data shows that about half of MSMs who have syphilis are also infected with HIV. MSMs are also 17 times more likely to get anal cancer.

All members of the LGBTQ community face a different set of risks of contracting STDs. Between 20 and 40 percent of homeless youth identify as LGBTQ and are more likely to have suffered from sexual abuse, drug and alcohol abuse, and mental health issues, which puts them at a much higher risk of developing an STD. Poverty and lack of family support also contribute to the likelihood of engaging in risky sexual behaviors. Social stigmas and homophobia can also make it hard for people in the LGBTQ community to get testing and treatment.

Long-Term Complications

In addition to problems associated with childbirth and a person's reproductive organs, STDs can lead to infection in other areas of the body as well. Rarely, gonorrhea can spread to the blood, heart, or joints, causing widespread infection and a life-threatening condition. If syphilis is not treated in its early stages, it can bring about serious long-term complications in men and women. Late-stage syphilis can cause brain

Teen STDs at Record Highs

About 40 percent of sexually active young women, aged 14 to 19, have an STD. According to the Centers for Disease Control and Prevention, this is partly due to the development of a woman's body. Adolescents and young women are more likely to contract STDs because the cervix has not fully matured, making them more susceptible to infection.

All young people, male and female, are at higher risk for STDs for other reasons as well. One reason is because they often fail to receive prevention services, perhaps due to a lack of insurance or the inability to pay. A lack of transportation, feeling uncomfortable with testing sites, and concerns about confidentiality are other reasons the CDC notes for higher rates among young people. Many young people are uncomfortable talking about sex openly and honestly, especially if they have had more than one partner.

The choices young people make also play into their high incidence of STDs. According to the CDC, of the U.S. high school students interviewed in 2015 who were sexually active, 43 percent did not use a condom the last time they had sex.

Finally, a lack of sex and HIV education in public schools is a contributing factor. Only 24 states and Washington, D.C., require public schools to teach sex education, and only 20 of those states require that the information is medically accurate. Additionally, only 33 states and Washington, D.C., require students to be taught about HIV/AIDS. Young people today also do not have the threat of a death sentence looming over them that previous generations did with HIV. "'There's a lack of fear,' says Dr. John Steever, an assistant professor of pediatrics at the Mount Sinai Adolescent Health Center in New York City. 'But that doesn't mean that an STD no longer can cause severe health complications,' adds Steever. 'That lack of forward-thinking is what we are running up against.'"[1]

1. Alexandra Sifferlin, "Here's Why Teen STDs Are Hitting All Time Highs," *TIME*, November 7, 2016. time.com/4558627/heres-why-teen-stds-are-hitting-all-time-highs/.

damage, cardiovascular and other organ damage, and death.

STDs can also lead to infertility in men. For instance, bacteria from the STDs chlamydia and gonorrhea can cause epididymitis, which is a painful infection in the tissue around the testicles. It can be treated with antibiotics, but the disease can bring on scarring that may lead to infertility.

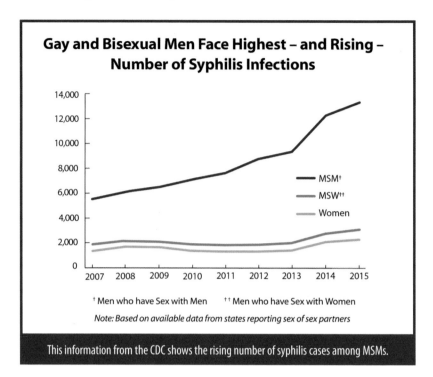

Gay and Bisexual Men Face Highest – and Rising – Number of Syphilis Infections

† Men who have Sex with Men   †† Men who have Sex with Women

Note: Based on available data from states reporting sex of sex partners

This information from the CDC shows the rising number of syphilis cases among MSMs.

The Link Between STDs and HIV

Another serious concern is that a person who already has an STD is more likely to also become infected with HIV. According to the CDC, syphilis is closely linked to HIV, especially among men. A Florida study showed that among men who had syphilis in 2003 but were not infected by HIV, 22 percent of them were diagnosed with HIV by 2011. People with HSV-2 (the herpes simplex virus that causes genital herpes) are three times as likely to develop HIV.

A person with any STD has a higher chance of getting HIV because the STD breaks down the body's natural barriers that provide infection protection. The sores and microscopic tears and skin abrasions associated with many STDs make it easier for HIV to enter the body. "It's like when you have allergies and your respiratory tract is irritated so you're more likely to catch a cold,"[10] Dr. Jill Grimes explained.

The Shock of Diagnosis

In addition to the physical impact of an STD, there is an emotional toll. "Richard" wrote that telling his family that he was HIV positive was "maybe even still the hardest thing I have ever done. My mother cried like I had never seen. My father couldn't even look or talk to me. My grandmother gave me a hug and my grandfather told me I had broken my father's heart."[11] When Anthony L. Contreras learned he tested positive for HIV, he could not think straight. "There was this wave of shock that kind of paralyzes you, then there's a flood of different thoughts that go through your mind lightning fast," he said. As the reality of the disease set in, he began to doubt his self-worth. "There's a feeling of being damaged goods, a feeling you'll never be loved," he said. "Are people going to judge me? Turn their backs on me?"[12]

Being diagnosed with an STD can bring on feelings of being alone and unwanted. It is not unusual for a person to experience shock and dismay at such a diagnosis. "When a person finds out she has genital warts it can be devastating," Grimes noted. "They think, 'How would anyone ever want to be with me?'"[13] When Maria learned she had herpes at age 21, she sat in her room, crying in disbelief. She said, "There was a feeling of 'Who's going to want me now?' There was embarrassment." It was not until she went to counseling that she began to heal emotionally. "It helped me realize that I'm not the only person out there with an STD,"[14] she said.

Although it is unsettling to be diagnosed with an STD, a person can learn to live with the disease. Some STDs can be easily cured, and incurable ones can be managed through treatment. Sometimes the diagnosis is more difficult to deal with than the disease itself. An anonymous person who has herpes shared their personal story on the American Sexual Health

Association's website: "If I had a magic wand I would get rid of herpes stigma. I would do this even before I'd use the magic wand to create a herpes cure. This infection rarely cause[s] me any trouble. I've had flea bites that hurt worse than an outbreak. What I suffer from is people's [judgment] and ignorance … I used to get angry by the rejection. It's a very small risk … at an infection … that causes mild symptoms! But what [people] really risk is catching something that stigmatizes them. They don't want to catch the stigma. No one wants to suffer from the stigma, and it's the stigma we need to fight … Don't be ashamed! You're still as good and worthy and beautiful as you were before."[15]

Being diagnosed with an STD can be a wake-up call, making a person more responsible about his or her decisions regarding sexual activity. It often makes a person lose the feeling of invulnerability and realize that he or she is not immune, noted sex educator Susan Cohen. "STDs have a huge emotional impact on young people," she said. "Unfortunately, it's that first STD that really gets a person to slow down and say, 'This can really happen to me.'"[16]

CHAPTER TWO

SCREENING AND DIAGNOSIS

Sara recalled a time in her mid-20s, when she lived in a small, Idaho town with little to do: "I worked and spent my spare time in the bars partying. I didn't have a steady boyfriend, but there were a few guys I'd hook up with. Mostly we'd use condoms for birth control, but sometimes—usually due to drinking, we had unprotected sex. I thought condoms were for birth control; I didn't even think about getting an STD."[17]

Sara remembers a stranger arriving to town. She was having breakfast in a diner after a night of partying and the man joined her and her friends. Because Sara was still too drunk to drive, the stranger drove her home and they had sex. Later she found out he gave her genital warts.

Sara says, "Now I look back and think, how could a college educated person like myself, lack so much knowledge? I didn't even know about STDs. I didn't even visit a doctor for 5 years! In a small town you know everyone, so I wasn't about to go to one of the three town doctors for birth control or for STD/HIV testing. One doctor had asked me out, one was super religious and I worked with the wife of the only remaining doc in town, so there was no way!"[18]

There are many reasons that people do not get tested for STDs right away. Sara admits she was embarrassed and ashamed, which kept her from getting diagnosed and treated. In other cases, people do not even know they have an STD, and some may have no noticeable signs or symptoms. Some STDs, if not treated, can have debilitating effects on the infected person's health. That is why it is so important for anyone who is sexually active to visit their doctor regularly and get tested for STDs.

Some STDs show no noticeable signs or syymptoms, which is why it is important for all sexually active people to be regularly checked for STDs.

Signs of a Problem

When a person has become infected with an STD, sometimes visible symptoms make that infection apparent. Symptoms of various STDs include warts, blisters, painful urination, or unusual discharge. The lymph nodes may also swell when a person has an STD. Lymph nodes are small, bean-shaped organs that are found at various places in the body. They are part of the body's immune system and help fight infection. When a person has an STD, nodes in the neck, armpits, and groin may swell. Swollen lymph nodes, however, may also be an indication of an illness that has nothing to do with an STD; therefore, a person should check with a doctor for the cause of this symptom.

One warning sign that should always be checked out by a doctor is unusual discharge from the vagina or penis. The STD chlamydia, for example, may cause a woman to experience abnormal vaginal discharge or bleeding in between periods. Gonorrhea may also cause a woman to have a yellowish discharge. Although it is not uncommon for women to have some clear, odorless discharge from the vagina, if it starts looking different or there is pain, odor, or itching to go along with it, she should see a doctor.

Discharge is also a symptom of STDs in men. A man with chlamydia may have discharge from the penis (generally seen in the morning, before he goes to the bathroom for the first time). The STD gonorrhea may also cause discharge that is white, yellow, or green. "Discharge from the penis is never a normal occurrence, and any man experiencing this symptom should be examined by a health care provider while he is having this symptom,"[19] noted physician Lisa Marr.

Other STD symptoms in men can include burning while urinating, pain, itching, and irritation inside the penis. These symptoms either may be constant or may come and go, and they indicate that a man should see a doctor.

In both men and women, certain STDs may cause sores or bumps to appear on a person's genitals. Genital warts are one of the most common symptoms of an STD. These flesh-colored bumps on the skin, which are caused by certain strains of the human papillomavirus (HPV), are harder than the surrounding skin and can be flat or raised. Few or many bumps may appear, and they can be small or large in size. Herpes may also announce itself with red or pimple-like bumps in the genital area. Classic genital herpes lesions are painful blisters or ulcers on the genitals. In some cases, people with gonorrhea also notice sores in the genital area, where painful pimples may appear. Although a rash in the genital area may be a sign of an STD, it may indicate an unrelated infection. "When a person notices a rash, sores or lesions, he or she should see a health care provider as soon as possible after the symptoms start, since the appearance of a rash may change over time and seeing the rash as soon as possible helps the health care provider make the correct diagnosis,"[20] Marr noted.

Sometimes an STD causes an infection that is not in the genital area. A person who performs oral sex is at risk for getting gonorrhea or chlamydia in the throat. Syphilis can also be transmitted during oral sex. A sign of this infection could be a sore throat, although many other infections also cause this symptom.

Asymptomatic STDs

Most people with HPV are asymptomatic, meaning they show no signs of infection. It is possible to have an STD without showing any symptoms at all. It may also take years for symptoms to present themselves. For these reasons, some STDs are called "silent"

Many people believe that if they do not have physical symptoms, they do not have to worry about an STD, but some STDs do not show symptoms for months.

diseases. A person may have them—and infect others— without realizing it. However, just because a sexually active person does not show signs of having an STD does not mean he or she is not infected.

The signs and symptoms of STDs can also be the same as the signs and symptoms of other illnesses, sometimes making it a challenge for doctors to diagnose them. Syphilis, for example, is called "the great imitator" because its symptoms often mimic the symptoms of other diseases. People may not realize that their sores are due to syphilis during the disease's first and second stages. People with gonorrhea can be infected for months before any symptoms occur.

When Infection Spreads

Sometimes a sexually transmitted infection is not noticed right away, and the infection spreads. When it spreads to a woman's reproductive organs, the impact is serious. The infection can cause pelvic inflammatory disease (PID). Two common causes of PID are chlamydia and gonorrhea; almost half of women with untreated chlamydia develop PID. The bacteria from these STDs cause inflammation of the cervix, and this then spreads to the uterus, fallopian tubes, and ovaries. Pelvic inflammatory disease affects about 5 percent of all women in the United States. It can cause infertility in about 8 percent of women each year, as PID can scar the fallopian tubes and block the release of eggs. It can also lead to ectopic pregnancy, a life-threatening condition in which a fertilized egg grows outside the uterus, generally in a fallopian tube.

The most common symptom of PID is pain in the lower abdomen that is often felt as a dull ache. Other symptoms include pain during intercourse, abnormal discharge, spotting between periods, heavier-than-usual periods, chills, fever, and nausea. Because the symptoms of PID may be mild and vary from person to person, it can be difficult for a health care provider to diagnose. Once a diagnosis is made, PID can be treated with antibiotics.

PID is an especially troubling issue for young women. PID is most commonly diagnosed in women between the ages of 15 and 24. A person who has sex with multiple partners increases her chances of getting PID, and a woman who has had it once is at higher risk of getting it again. "A single episode of PID changes the anatomy of the pelvic organs, so that a woman is at higher risk for developing PID again if she is infected with this bacteria,"[21] Marr wrote. Other risk factors include douching, which can push bacteria further into the reproductive organs, and intrauterine devices (IUDs), which are a kind of birth control that is placed inside the uterus.

Serious Side Effects

It is not only women who may become infertile if chlamydia or gonorrhea progresses to a more serious infection. Men run the risk of getting epididymitis, an infection that can lead to infertility.

Epididymitis is an inflammation of the epididymis, which is a tube that sits at the back of the testicles. Signs include discharge and burning while urinating, swelling, and pain. The swelling and pain generally occur on one side. Other signs may be that half the scrotum is swollen, hot, and painful. The infection can be treated with antibiotics.

Other STDs can progress to serious conditions as well. Syphilis is curable, but if it is not treated, it can bring about serious long-term problems. These complications include brain, cardiovascular, and organ damage as well as death.

A sore in the primary stage of the disease can progress to a rough, reddish rash, which may not itch. These last three to six weeks and heal whether they are treated or not. Symptoms of the second stage of the disease can include fever, swollen glands, sore throat, fatigue, skin rashes, and lesions in the mouth, vagina, or anus. The symptoms of this stage of syphilis will also go away without being treated. Without treatment, syphilis progresses to its latent stage, in which the disease may hide for years. The infection is still in the body, however, and can progress to the late stages of the disease, which can cause serious medical problems such as damage to a person's brain and heart, as well as blindness, dementia, and paralysis.

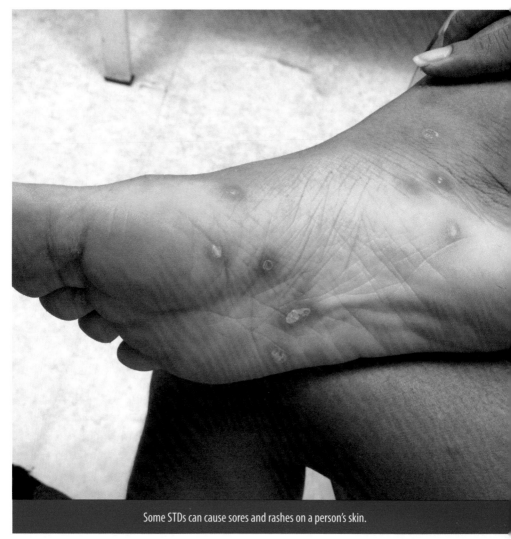

Some STDs can cause sores and rashes on a person's skin.

The virus that causes genital herpes can also go into a latent state. The herpes simplex virus (HSV-1 or HSV-2) is still present in the body during the latent state, but it does not produce infectious particles. Over time, the number of outbreaks a person experiences may decrease, but this does not mean that the body is free of the virus. Another outbreak of sores may occur at any time and generally appear during times of stress.

Outbreaks of herpes are considered more of a nuisance, but HPV can progress to a life-threatening stage. Although the majority of HPV viruses are naturally cleared by a person's immune system, HPV is the number one cause of oropharyngeal cancer (cancer at the very back of the mouth and part of the throat) and some other oral cancers. HPV16 is the strain most associated with oral, penis, and anus cancers, and it is the cause of almost all cases of cervical cancer. Someone can have HPV for years and never know it because the virus does not always produce a noticeable symptom. There also is generally no way of a person knowing how long ago they may have been infected with HPV. A person can have it for decades before cancer develops.

How STD Testing Works

Testing for STDs gives a person a good chance of detecting the disease early and receiving proper treatment. Even without the visible signs of an STD, a person can carry the disease in his or her body and still may be able to spread it to others. Urine tests, blood tests, and swab tests are all used by doctors when testing patients for STDs.

A urine test, for example, is used to see if a person has chlamydia. A person gives a urine sample, and it is examined in a lab for signs of chlamydia bacteria. A urine test may also be used to see if a person has

When Should Someone Get Tested?

A person should see a doctor if he or she has obvious symptoms such as discharge, burning during urination, or an unusual sore or rash. If these symptoms occur, the person needs to stop having sex and seek treatment. A person who has been diagnosed and is being treated for an STD should tell his or her sex partner immediately about the diagnosis so he or she can also seek treatment. Telling that person can help stop the spread of the disease and prevent that person from developing serious complications if the disease is not treated.

Even if someone is not showing symptoms, the CDC recommends regular screening for certain people. They state that everyone between 13 and 64 should have an HIV test. Sexually active women under the age of 25 should be tested annually for chlamydia and gonorrhea as well as older women with new or multiple sex partners. The CDC also recommends that all sexually active gay, bisexual, and other MSMs should be screened yearly for gonorrhea, syphilis, and chlamydia, and MSMs with multiple or anonymous partners should be screened every three to six months. Screening for syphilis, HIV, chlamydia, and gonorrhea is recommended for all pregnant women as early in the pregnancy as possible. Anyone who has regular, unsafe sex should be screened at least once a year.

gonorrhea. Some clinics and doctors' offices can do a Gram stain to test for gonorrhea. This test, which works better for men than women, involves taking a sample from the urethra or cervix. The sample is placed on a slide and is stained with dye before it is examined under a microscope. A doctor then looks for bacteria in the sample.

A swab test is another test that can be used by doctors to check for chlamydia and gonorrhea. With a swab test, a sample is taken from the cervix, penis, or other infected area. The sample is then analyzed in a laboratory. If a patient's symptoms include sores, a sample may be taken from a sore to test for the STD. A health care provider will generally diagnose herpes in this manner. A person can also be tested for syphilis by having a health care provider test fluid from syphilis sores. Genital warts caused by HPV are generally diagnosed visually. Sexually active women should have regular Pap tests that can help detect whether the cells in her cervix are changing and becoming cancerous. If a Pap result is abnormal, a biopsy and an HPV test may be done, since HPV can lead to cervical cancer.

A blood test is another tool doctors use to screen for certain STDs. A blood test can be used for both HIV and syphilis. The blood test can detect antibodies that the body produces after a person is infected.

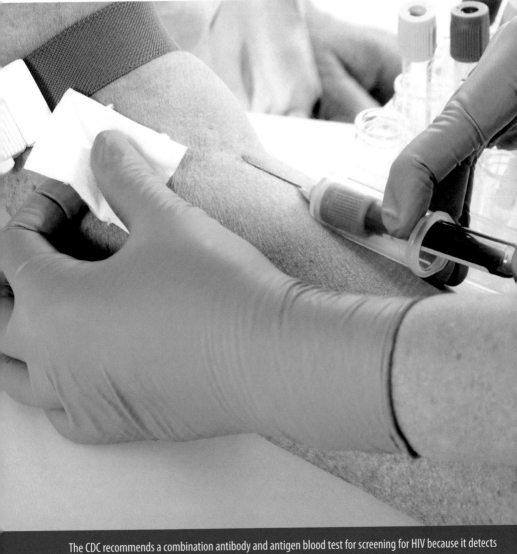

The CDC recommends a combination antibody and antigen blood test for screening for HIV because it detects the virus 20 days earlier than other tests, and doctors can get the results in about 20 minutes.

Why Should I Get Tested?

Most people believe that they would know if they had an STD, but that is not true. Many have mild symptoms that could be mistaken for something else or no symptoms at all. While certain groups are at a higher risk for contracting STDs than others, there are good reasons for everyone to get tested.

Many STDs can be transferred by skin-to-skin contact, which means even people who have not had sexual intercourse can get STDs. STDs can also be spread by oral sex. People in monogamous relationships for years generally think they are safe, but since some STDs can lay dormant for years, screening is still important.

Another reason to get tested is peace of mind. Worrying about getting a disease is sometimes worse than knowing that there was a positive diagnosis for the disease. Many people find that after they have been diagnosed they feel a sense of relief, because at least now they know what is wrong with their bodies and how to treat them. Also, earlier detection of STDs makes them much easier to treat.

Bacterial STDs

With a positive STD test result, a person may learn that the infection is curable. Bacterial STDs can be easily treated with antibiotics if they are detected early enough. Two common bacterial STDs, chlamydia and gonorrhea, can be successfully cured with antibiotics. A single dose is often all that is needed to cure them. Many people who have gonorrhea also have chlamydia and can take antibiotics for both diseases simultaneously.

However, in some cases, gonorrhea may be more difficult to treat. A person who has a strain of gonorrhea that is resistant to some classes of drugs can work with his or her doctor to find a medication that works.

Current Gonorrhea Treatment Losing Effectiveness

According to research presented by the National Center for HIV/AIDS, Viral Hepatitis, STD, and TB Prevention at the 2016 STD Prevention Conference in Atlanta, Georgia, the current recommended treatment of gonorrhea is losing its effectiveness. "Our last line of defense against gonorrhea is weakening," said Dr. Jonathan Mermin. "If resistance continues to increase and spread, current treatment will ultimately fail and 800,000 Americans a year will be at risk for untreatable gonorrhea."[1]

The CDC recommends dual therapy to treat gonorrhea that includes a shot of ceftriaxone and an oral dose of azithromycin. Over many years, gonorrhea has become resistant to most other antibiotics, and now new studies show that people may be becoming resistant to these drugs as well. "The whole reliance on antibiotics in our world has become an issue," said Susan Cohen. "We take pills for everything. We're now seeing some antibiotic-resistant strains."[2]

In the past, when gonorrhea developed a resistance to an antibiotic, the CDC would revise its treatment and recommend another antibiotic. Now, however, there are not any reliable or affordable backup medications available. CDC researchers are working on a new antibiotic (ETX0914) to replace the ceftriaxone, and early results have been promising. "Our research team and study participants take the possibility of untreatable gonorrhea very seriously," said Stephanie N. Taylor, M.D., professor of medicine and microbiology at Louisiana State University Health Sciences Center and the trial's lead investigator. "We are very pleased with these results and look forward to seeing ETX0914 advance through additional clinical studies."[3] The CDC still recommends the current dual therapy treatment because it works in most cases; however, any treatment failure should be reported to the CDC.

Shown here is a type of bacteria that causes gonorrhea.

1. Quoted in National Center for HIV/AIDS, Viral Hepatitis, STD, and TB Prevention, "New Warning Signs that Gonorrhea Treatment May be Losing Effectiveness," CDC.gov, September 21, 2016. www.cdc.gov/nchhstp/newsroom/2016/2016-std-prevention-conference-press-release.html.

2. Susan Cohen, telephone interview by author of *Sexually Transmitted Diseases*, April 24, 2009.

3. Quoted in National Center for HIV/AIDS, Viral Hepatitis, STD, and TB Prevention, "New Warning Signs that Gonorrhea Treatment May be Losing Effectiveness."

To help prevent the disease from becoming resistant to more drugs, a person being treated for gonorrhea should take all recommended medication.

It is easy to treat and cure syphilis when the disease is in its early stages. To treat the disease, a person receives an intramuscular injection of penicillin from a health care professional. The duration of treatment varies, depending on the stage of the disease. For people who have had syphilis for longer than a year, more doses of penicillin will be needed. If a person is allergic to penicillin, other antibiotics are available to treat the disease. The treatment kills syphilis bacteria and prevents further damage. However, if a person's brain, heart, or other organs have been damaged by syphilis, it will not repair the damage that has already been done by the disease.

Viral STDs

Viral STDs cannot be cured, but their symptoms can often be controlled with medication. Genital herpes is one STD for which no cure exists. However, people with herpes can take antiviral medications that make outbreaks of the sores shorter and can even prevent them in some patients. The treatment differs for the first time a person has a herpes outbreak, for an acute outbreak, and for long-term suppression of the disease. A person who has more than six occurrences in a year may benefit from taking medication daily to suppress the virus.

HPV, which causes genital warts and can lead to cervical cancer, also can be treated but not cured. However, 90 percent of HPV infections are cleared within 12 to 24 months by the body's immune system. A person who gets genital warts can treat them with a medicated cream or can have them surgically removed through freezing or burning. Genital warts often go away on their own, although the virus remains in a person's body.

HIV rates in the United States have decreased in the past decade. The number of new diagnoses between 2005 and 2014 has declined 19 percent. Shown here is an illustration of an HIV infection.

Genital warts are only one condition brought on by HPV, which has more than 100 subtypes. Although some subtypes cause no health problems, others cause genital warts or cervical cancer. Certain types of HPV bring about cervical cancer when they cause abnormal cells to divide and grow out of control at the opening to the uterus. If the disease is caught early, 92 percent of people survive for at least 5 years after the cancer is found. Treatment for cervical cancer depends on the stage of the disease. Common treatments include surgery, radiation, and chemotherapy.

Another STD that can be treated but not cured is HIV, which attacks a person's immune system and causes AIDS. HIV is constantly changing and quickly becomes resistant to drugs. However, there is medication to slow the progression of the disease. There is also medication called pre-exposure prophylaxis (PrEP), which can be taken by people who are HIV negative but are considered high-risk to prevent them from getting HIV. Today, treatments for people with HIV allow them to live years longer than they would have been able to in the past. Nonetheless, HIV remains a major health threat in the United States.

A Vicious Cycle

Sometimes a person who has received treatment for a curable STD will continue to experience symptoms or test positive for the STD. This means the person has been reinfected. Researchers believe that up to 20 percent of gonorrhea and chlamydia cases are reinfections.

To prevent reinfection, a person's sex partners should also be treated for the STD, even if they do not show symptoms. They should abstain from sex until both treatments have ended. Finishing the prescribed antibiotic therapy is important. The symptoms may go away in a few days, but unless the entire series of medication is taken, the bacteria could return.

If symptoms do not go away within one or two weeks after a person has finished taking medication, he or she should see the doctor again. The CDC also advises women to be retested for chlamydia three or four months after receiving treatment. This is especially important if a person's sex partner has not been treated or if a person has sex with a new partner.

It is especially important for women to be retested after receiving treatment because serious problems can develop if a woman is reinfected. A woman who is reinfected is at a higher risk for reproductive health issues, including infertility.

As Berman noted, "This is a case of sometimes what you don't know can hurt you."[22]

Telling a sexual partner about the disease so they can be treated is not always an easy step. The CDC implemented a program called Expedited Partner Therapy (EPT) in an effort to encourage people to have their partners treated. While referring the partner to another doctor is the best practice, there are many reasons that may prevent them from going. The EPT program allows the partner of an infected person to receive treatment without being identified or having an STD test. The CDC considers it an effective program, but it is controversial. Four states have banned the program, and many insurance companies are against it, saying that it doubles the cost of treatment.

CHAPTER THREE

AFTER THE DIAGNOSIS

A 24-year-old veterinary technician shared her story about being diagnosed with chlamydia: "I just found out yesterday, but I've probably had it for about 4–6 months. That's about the time frame I was intimate with my ex … who apparently, had been unfaithful with his ex-girlfriend while we were together."[23] She talked about how having an STD has affected her current relationship: "I told him immediately since we had sexual intercourse for the first time 3 days ago. He was in shock, didn't say much, and I don't blame him. I felt the exact same way when I found out. I haven't heard from him since I told him earlier today … Even though he knows it's not my fault, he just can't shake the fact that I gave him an STD."[24]

For most people, an STD diagnosis will change their lives and the lives of people they are close with. For many, it will be a shameful, humiliating experience. Some become depressed. However, others have used their diagnosis to help make positive changes in other people's lives. Jenelle Marie Pierce wrote,

I've lived with genital herpes for 14 years. In that time, I've learned how to have effective conversations with potential partners, I've learned that my STD does not define me, I've gained strength and open-mindedness, I've learned how to choose trustworthy friendships and prosperous relationships, and I've become an advocate for those living with an STD and all people who have experienced adversity. Those lessons came with a lot – A LOT – of trial and error – emphasis on the error as well and were all a result of contracting herpes. Consequently, removing my herpes would make me a much less interesting individual and I'd be afraid that I'd still be the incredibly shallow and naïve person I once was.[25]

Maria: "I Was Beside Myself"

STDs were the farthest thing from Maria's mind when she felt attracted to a good-looking guy in one of her college classes. She was always happy when he would meet her and her friends out at popular nightspots. Before long, it became apparent that the attraction was mutual.

One night, they went home together. One thing led to another, and they had sexual intercourse. They used protection, and Maria had no concern that their night together would lead to a sexually transmitted infection. She never thought that night would be the beginning of a lifelong herpes infection for her.

Maria had no idea that her partner had herpes or that she could get the genital herpes virus even if her partner used protection. (The herpes virus can spread if the sores are not covered by a condom and can also spread even if the sores are not present.) "I was twenty-one and you think you're invincible," she said. "I hadn't been promiscuous. It can happen to anyone and that's why I wanted to share my story."[26]

Several days later, Maria realized something was wrong. When she went to the bathroom, it hurt to urinate. Her joints got sore, and her knees ached. "I could barely walk down stairs," she said. "I was in excruciating pain."[27]

When she felt a tingling in her genital area and saw the sores, she knew she had become infected with herpes. The signs were readily apparent. "I didn't even really need to go to the doctor, but I did," she said. "I went to an urgent care clinic, and she did a biopsy of a sore."[28]

A few days later the doctor called to confirm Maria's suspicions. Even though Maria had already known that this was the case, the emotional impact of hearing that she had herpes was horrible. "I was beside myself," she said. "I cried; I sat in my room and bawled my eyes out for a good amount of time."[29]

Maria needed someone to confide in, and she turned to her mother for support. She told her about her condition and the pain she was having. Together, she and her mother went to see Maria's gynecologist to find out what could be done.

Maria learned that her condition could not be cured, but medication could make the outbreaks less severe. She began taking a medication called Valtrex, and she continues to take it every day to suppress the effect of the infection. "Some people take it only when they're having an outbreak coming on," Maria said. "I wanted to avoid it altogether."[30]

In addition to Valtrex, Maria has found lysine tablets can help shorten the duration of the outbreaks. She also learned that stress and a lack of sleep can bring on an outbreak. As a college student, she did not always get enough rest, but she did her best. "The first outbreak was probably one of the worst; they've gotten better since then," said Maria. "The first year was pretty hard. I probably had one outbreak a month. Now it's very mild, more of an inconvenience."[31]

Whereas medication has helped make Maria's physical symptoms less severe, seeing a therapist has helped make living with the disease less emotionally painful. The therapist emphasized to Maria that she is far from the only person who has the infection. Maria also realized her fear that no man would ever find her attractive was unfounded, and she entered into a stable relationship.

Because of her initial emotional distress and fears, Maria wanted to tell others what her experience has been like. The disease can happen to anyone, she noted, no matter how careful he or she may be. "I wanted to share my story because ... there's a stigma," she says. "I've told a couple of my closest friends, and they say you never would think that would happen to you, you're so careful."[32]

Maria still knows people who do not use protection and do not seem to be worried about catching an STD. She wants them to realize that the threat is out there, even though it is not openly discussed often enough. "People don't talk about it, and the doctor made me realize that it happens more often than not, unfortunately," [33] Maria said.

Being diagnosed with an STD can cause depression. Getting therapy or sharing the experience with others with STDs can help people cope with their diagnosis.

Kelly: Herpes Is a "Nonissue"

Kelly is 36 years old, the mother of a 2-year-old with another baby on the way, and has been dealing with herpes for 20 years. The infection is part of her life, but she has not let it hold her back from having a happy marriage and family life. "It happened and I'm dealing with it," she said. "Everything is going well. I sometimes forget that I even have it."[34]

Because she takes precautions, Kelly is not worried that her herpes will have an impact on the health of her children or husband. She has not let it control the way she lives her life, and this includes the way she has approached pregnancy and childbirth. When she prepared to give birth to her first child, she talked with her doctor about what she should do so she could give birth vaginally, rather than by cesarean section, to avoid the risk of transmitting herpes to her baby. A mother having a herpes outbreak at the time of delivery risks infecting the child, so to reduce this chance Kelly took daily medication 45 days before her due date to lessen her risk of having an outbreak. When the day of her daughter's birth arrived, Kelly was not having an outbreak and was able to give birth vaginally. Her daughter was not infected and remains healthy. Kelly plans to have a vaginal birth for her second child also, unless an outbreak occurs shortly before her baby is due to arrive.

Kelly's husband also remains uninfected, and they abstain from sex when she feels an outbreak coming on. "It's being honest. If I feel a little of a sensation that may be an outbreak, I'm going to play it safe so I don't get my partner sick," she said. "Sometimes it turns into nothing, but I'd rather be safe than sorry."[35]

Herpes has been such a common part of her life for so long that she was shocked when a teenage female relative was not supported by her parents when they learned she had herpes. The girl and her family were broken up about the disease, Kelly said, and were also misinformed about the implications of the disease, telling the girl that having herpes would negatively affect any romantic relationship she ever has. The young girl was also embarrassed by her partner sharing the news of her infection with others at their school, and she was scared rather than comforted by her parents because of their misunderstanding about the disease.

Their reaction and lack of knowledge about the disease prompted Kelly to stress that a person with herpes is not defined by the disease and can have a rich and fulfilling life. "Yes, I regret that I have this but it hasn't ruined my life," she said. "It's really important for a young person who may feel self-conscious or vulnerable to have good access to information about what this means in their life."[36]

Gathering information about the condition helped Kelly deal with herpes after she was diagnosed with the disease. She was 20 and in college when she learned she had genital herpes, but the news did not scare her, as she already suspected that something was amiss. "I wasn't shocked or depressed because, maybe without even knowing it, I had been dealing with it for a couple years,"[37] she said.

She suspects she became infected while she was in high school. At age 16, she was in a steady relationship. Because she was using birth control, she felt it would be all right to have sex without a condom. As far as Kelly knew, the relationship was monogamous, but she later learned her boyfriend had been having sex with another girl. While in high school, she broke out with painful blisters on her genitals, a symptom of herpes. "Shortly after I found out that he had been spending time with someone else, I had my first outbreak," she said. "It was a typical first outbreak, very painful, but I didn't know what it was and it went away."[38]

The disease did not flare up severely enough to cause her to seek medical treatment for several years, and after she was diagnosed, Kelly was determined not to infect anyone else. If her boyfriend had been honest with her, she reasoned, she could have been spared the sometimes-painful condition. She learned more about the infection and made sure anyone she became romantically involved with was also educated. She was honest about her condition, made sure her partner used a condom when they had intercourse, and did not have intercourse when she had an outbreak or suspected one was coming on. Kelly explained:

> *I got pamphlets and brochures to help understand it. Anytime I was spending time with a man and thought there was the potential for romantic involvement, I had this brochure I would give him. I would tell him that I had herpes, and that I understood if the information scared him. I would give him the brochure and let him read it. No one freaked out, no one was scared by it or really weirded out by it. Open communication has helped me avoid getting other people sick.*[39]

Kelly has come to terms with living with her condition and what she must do to keep from infecting others. Although having herpes is not an ideal situation, she wanted others to know that a person with a herpes infection can live a normal life. "Herpes has not negatively affected [my life] in any major way," she said. "It's almost like a nonissue."[40]

Michelle: "You Cannot Take It Back"

Michelle did not know what the human papillomavirus (HPV) was when she was in high school. She did not realize that HPV would lead her to develop cervical cancer and ultimately take away her ability to become pregnant.

STDs and Infants

Babies whose mothers have STDs are at risk for many life-threatening problems. Mothers can pass STDs on to their children during pregnancy or childbirth.

A pregnant woman with chlamydia, for example, may have complications including pre-term labor and low birth weight. She could also pass her disease on to the baby during childbirth. This can result in the baby getting an eye infection that can cause blindness if untreated. A newborn can also contract pneumonia, characterized by congestion and a cough that worsens.

A pregnant woman who has gonorrhea is at risk for miscarriage or delivering a preterm baby. A baby infected with gonorrhea can become blind or have a joint or blood infection. The blood infection can be life threatening.

If a pregnant woman gives the herpes simplex virus to her newborn, the baby may develop neonatal HSV, which is rare but can be fatal. A pregnant woman with syphilis puts her baby at risk for complications ranging from developmental delays and seizures to death. The baby may die shortly after birth, or a woman may give birth to a stillborn baby. An infected baby may be born with no signs of the disease initially, but after a few weeks, he or she can develop serious problems if not treated immediately. Because of the severe complications that can occur, it is recommended that every pregnant woman be tested for syphilis.

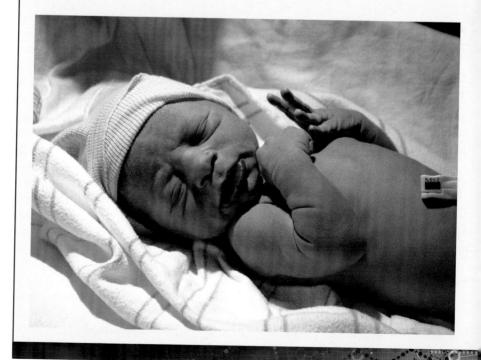

Michelle had her first sexual experience at age 14, not realizing that sex put her at risk for getting HPV, which can lead to cervical cancer. "At such a young age we don't know all the facts or consequences," she said. "I can't say who I got HPV from and it doesn't matter, but I do know that at sixteen I went to the gynecologist for the first time, and at seventeen I had a second Pap test and had an abnormal Pap."[41]

The Pap test checks for changes in the cells of the cervix, which is in the lower part of the uterus. Cells in the cervix may change from normal to precancerous and then to cancerous, and a Pap test is done to see if any changes are occurring. The abnormal cell growth can be caused by HPV.

Michelle was found to have abnormal cells in her cervix. To remove them, her cervix was frozen to kill the abnormal cells through cryosurgery. "After that they followed me pretty closely," she said. "I had Pap tests every three months for a year, and then every six months for another year."[42]

The Pap tests were done to screen for more abnormal cells, and after two years of normal Pap tests, she went back to having an annual screening. Then, at age 25, Michelle began to notice itching in her genitals. A biopsy showed that she had a precancerous condition of the vulva, a woman's external genitals. The precancerous condition can be caused by HPV. To treat the condition, the abnormal cells were burned off of the vulva during laser surgery. "It was extremely painful," Michelle says. "Today I know that the cell changes were the direct result of the HPV infection, but at the time I wasn't educated enough to know that."[43]

The next year, during a routine exam, she was tested for HPV and also had a Pap test to check for abnormal cells in her cervix. Although the Pap was normal, she tested positive for a type of HPV that is linked to cervical cancer. Additional exams and biopsies revealed that she had cervical cancer. Michelle researched her options and had surgery that would remove her cervix but still leave her with a chance of having children one day. The surgery was successful, and for two years, Michelle's cancer went into remission.

Three days after her boyfriend proposed, however, Michelle had another checkup and learned that her battle with cancer was not over. The cancer had returned, and she would require more surgery. "I went from the highest high to the lowest low in the universe,"[44] she said.

She knew she would need to undergo surgery and other treatments for her cancer. Still hoping to have children, she underwent a procedure that removed some of her eggs from her ovaries. Ten days after getting married, she had surgery to remove her uterus and other reproductive organs. To kill the cancerous cells, she also had radiation and chemotherapy.

The cancer treatment was not easy on Michelle. The chemotherapy made her feel nauseated, and it made her feel queasy just to smell food cooking. The radiation was even harder on her body. Her husband comforted her by simply rubbing her feet or head while she had her chemotherapy treatments. "It was a crazy experience, but it taught me what real love is about," Michelle said. "Sex is something we do, but there are so many other ways you can be intimate and show somebody you love them."[45]

While she was in college, Michelle had written a research paper on cervical cancer. It was around this time she had her first cancer surgery, and she was amazed to find how little people knew about HPV and cervical cancer. "I was utterly amazed at the lack of knowledge," she said. "They hadn't heard of HPV. Most of them had no idea of the risk factors."[46]

That is when she decided she would not keep her cancer a secret and would use her story to try to educate other women. She now speaks to groups about cervical cancer.

High-Risk HPV

According to the National Cancer Institute (NCI), there were an estimated 12,820 new cases of cervical cancer diagnosed in 2017. These numbers are down by half from what they were 30 years ago, and survival rates have increased every year for the past 10 years. This is because the Pap test, which looks for cell changes on the cervix, is now recommended for every woman between the ages of 21 and 65. Cervical cancer is one of the easiest cancers to treat as long as it is detected early.

The cervix is located in the lower part of a woman's uterus. It connects the uterus, which is where a fetus grows, to the vagina, or birth canal. Almost all cervical cancers start from a high-risk HPV infection. Most women's immune systems can get rid of the infection without her ever knowing there was a problem. However, 10 percent of women infected with high-risk HPV will be put at risk for cervical cancer.

To avoid getting HPV, the CDC recommends the following guidelines:

- Get the HPV vaccine. According to the CDC, the HPV vaccine is safe and effective and recommended for all boys and girls aged 11 to 12.

- A person should limit their number of sexual partners.

- A person should use condoms the right way every time they have sex.

- Do not smoke.

- Have regular screenings to find precancerous cells before it turns into cancer. The Pap test is the most common.

Pap tests are done during pelvic exams and are simple and quick. The doctor collects cells, such as the ones shown here, by swabbing the cervix with a special stick, and the cells are then sent to a lab for testing.

With the help of a surrogate mother, she was able to have a child. It has been a long and painful road to motherhood for her, and she wants others to know the implications of STDs. "These STDs are so rampant that you can have sex one time, with or without a condom, and you can get HPV or genital herpes and it will change your life forever. You cannot take it back," she said. "You always think it's going to happen to that girl, you know the one, the promiscuous girl, the one from the wrong side of the tracks, the one from the wrong neighborhood. It doesn't matter how pretty you are or wealthy you are or what family you come from, it happens to people from all walks of life. The truth is you can come from the best family, or be the smartest girl in school and you can still be that girl."[47]

Anthony: A Harsh World

When he was first diagnosed with HIV, there was no way Anthony L. Contreras could stop thinking about the disease. The reality was with him when he woke up, all through the day, and into the evening. Even if he wanted to try to forget for a little while, his pill regimen of two in the morning, two at midday, and two more before bed brought him back to reality.

"It was the first thing I had to think about in the morning and the last thing I had to think about before going to bed," he said. "It didn't allow me the chance to feel normal, which is, I think, what everyone wants."[48]

It took two years for Anthony to come to terms with his HIV-positive status. He eventually realized that he was much more than simply a person with HIV and that he had much to offer. However, before he began feeling worthy again, he went through a period of depression that made it a struggle just to get out of bed in the morning. He felt unloved and unwanted. "I was looking for love and acceptance and value, and I couldn't find it,"[49] he said.

Anthony gradually began to see himself as a person, not a virus. He got a job educating others about HIV and its prevention. When he talks to young people about the disease, however, he is sometimes surprised by the many misperceptions he encounters. Some worry that it can be transmitted through sweat (it cannot), and others think that girls do not get it (they can). Most unsettling is the notion he encounters that HIV is no longer a big deal because there are drugs and treatments for it, although Anthony knows all too well that the disease is incurable. "That's the difficult part,"[50] he said.

Anthony is well aware of the risk of having unprotected sex, even one time. At age 21, he had sex for the first time and insisted that his partner use a condom. His partner refused. Finally, Anthony gave in.

A few months later, Anthony realized something was not right when he became very sick. The next time he became ill, he went to a doctor and asked to be tested for "everything." "He asked if I was at risk for HIV, and I said yes," Anthony said. "He told me he had done hundreds of these tests and only two had ever been positive, so I didn't think anything about it that weekend. Then I got the call on Tuesday, and the doctor said the results showed that everything came back fine except for the HIV, which was positive."[51]

For a time, Anthony did not know what to think. His mind was flooded with thoughts as he wondered how this disease would impact his future and how he would ever tell his family. By now, his former partner wanted nothing more to do with him. "At twenty-one it was a slap in the face," Anthony said. "Sex is a very harsh world."[52]

Anthony came to realize that he could not let the virus overtake who he was as a person. He saw value in sharing the message that an HIV-positive person is so much more than simply someone with HIV. The virus does not change the fact that someone is still someone's son or daughter and has many valuable gifts to offer. "You are not a virus; you are a person,"[53] he said.

For the past decade, Anthony has lived with acceptance of his condition. He is proud of the work he does in HIV education and is supportive of the young people he meets and educates. "You really build this relationship and rapport with these kids who are looking for guidance and acceptance; just take an interest in them and care,"[54] he said.

Talking about safe sex with a partner well before having sex is important. A person is then less likely to take a risk and have sex without protection "just this once" while being intimate.

He still sees room for improvement, however, when it comes to dealing with people who learn they have HIV. "What is really missed and left out is the emotional strain it puts on you," he said. "There's a feeling you're damaged goods, a feeling you'll never be loved. Are people going to judge me? Turn their backs on me? Nobody thinks about any of that." There are implications of having HIV that people do not think of, he said, if they focus on treatment of the virus alone. "Even if there is treatment and education, there are other things factored in that you don't account for," he said. "How do you date somebody? I've been on a lot of really good first dates, but when it gets to the end of the night, I was getting, 'You should have told me sooner,' and that's really damaging."[55]

A message that teens often miss, he said, is that sex has implications. Teens often underestimate the risk of getting an STD, he said, and they also do not realize what a serious decision it is to have sex with someone. "You're opening the door not just to the emotional aspect of sex," he noted, "but all the disease that comes with it."[56]

Living with HIV

The human immunodeficiency virus (HIV) is the virus that causes AIDS, which is fatal if not treated. According to the CDC, more than 1.2 million people in the United States have HIV, but it is estimated that 13 percent do not know they have the disease. A total of 18,303 people became infected with AIDS in 2015.

Certain groups have a higher risk of acquiring HIV. Gay and bisexual men have higher HIV rates than heterosexual men. In 2014, gay and bisexual men made up 83 percent of the new HIV diagnoses among men 13 and older, and 67 percent of the total new diagnoses that same year. Black men and women, along with Latino men also have higher HIV rates than other ethnic groups.

Tom: An Uncomfortable Secret

A diagnosis of herpes can be unsettling and disturbing news, bringing emotional pain that exceeds the physical discomfort the disease causes. Tom, a 56-year-old father of two, was troubled and distressed after learning he was infected with genital herpes.

When his doctor first told him he had herpes, Tom could not believe what he was hearing. "I went to the doctor because I had what I thought was a callus," he said. "It looked like a callus to me. Then he ran the test and it wasn't a callus." The doctor explained that the herpes virus could have been dormant for years, appearing when triggered by stress or some other factor. "At first I didn't believe it, I just couldn't believe it," he said. "I went through the denial period and then I went through the blame period."[57]

The fact that he likely had herpes for years without knowing it was also upsetting for him. He believes it to be the result of a relationship he had more than a decade earlier when he was separated from his wife. After that relationship, he and the woman he had been involved with were both treated for chlamydia, which was quickly cured with an antibiotic, but he was not tested for other STDs. Tom's relationship with the woman ended, and he later reunited with his wife. For a while, he was afraid to have children because he feared he had another STD.

After no symptoms appeared, he thought everything was fine. He and his wife had another child, and Tom stopped thinking about STDs until the sore appeared.

The infection has not bothered him much physically. Medication taken when an outbreak begins controls the symptoms. However, the emotional aspect of the diagnosis is another matter. "It's been more of a mental thing than a physical thing," he said, noting that it is an unpleasant reminder of the separation from his wife. "I feel it's affected my relationship with my wife and my family," he said. "My wife says I'm not as loving as I used to be."[58]

The diagnosis is something he has not told others about. He cannot bring himself to mention it to his wife for fear of reopening the wounds of their previous separation. "I'm afraid if she gets tested she's going to have it," he said. "She's going to blame it on me, and that thing from ten years ago will pop back up. I'm afraid it will ruin my marriage if I bring it up." As he keeps the information inside, however, there is no denying that it is an uncomfortable secret he is keeping. "It's on my mind every day,"[59] he said.

CHAPTER FOUR

STOPPING THE SPREAD OF STDS

An anonymous person posted the following on the American Sexual Health Association's (ASHA) website:

> *I've been dating the same boy for 10 years. We've been together since we were 16. This is the boy I'm willing to marry; the only one I've ever loved. Two years ago, I met a man who was 12 years [older than me] and completely drove me crazy. For the first time in my life I was going to be unfaithful. We had unprotected intercourse. I perfectly knew it was a risk for my health but ... in those moments I did not care. In February this year I went on for my annual Pap test and I found out I have HPV. I did not know anything about this disease. That man gave it to me.[60]*

People have known about STDs and how they are transmitted for many years, yet they continue to spread. To understand this ongoing issue, one must go beyond what is known clinically about STDs and explore people's personal beliefs, experiences, and education regarding sex.

High Risk Behaviors

STDs do not discriminate. They can impact anyone who has sex—from the richest person on the block to someone struggling to pay for lunch—however, a person's decisions can put him or her at higher risk for getting an STD.

According to a 2014 study at the McKinley Health Center, 23 percent of sexually active teens said they had unprotected sex because they were using drugs or alcohol at the time. Forty-eight percent of all men and women who had sex after a night of drinking regretted the encounter.

Someone who has sex—either oral or vaginal—without using a condom is at higher risk for an STD. People are also at a higher risk of getting an STD if they have sex with someone who has sex with multiple partners. The younger a person is when they first have sex, the more at risk they are of getting an STD in their lifetime. Others at risk include people who inject drugs, people who have been diagnosed with other STDs, and sex workers.

Mixing drugs, alcohol, and sexual behavior is a dangerous business, as using drugs or drinking alcohol increases a person's risk for getting an STD. Because drinking and drugs impair judgment and decision-making, a person under their influence may do things that he or she normally would avoid. "People partying under the influence is a big issue," Susan Cohen said. "Maybe some of the safer sex guidelines they set for themselves are in their head somewhere, but when they're partying those guidelines are nowhere to be found."[61]

How STDs Spread

Although certain lifestyle choices put a person at a higher risk of getting an STD, the diseases themselves are caused by an infection. Sexual contact allows the infection to pass from one person to another. This infection can be carried by bacteria or by a virus living in certain body fluids. When a person has sex, these fluids are shared and the infection is spread.

Bacteria are the cause of STDs such as chlamydia and gonorrhea, which can be treated and cured. The gonorrhea bacteria thrive in the warm and moist areas of a person's reproductive tract. The bacteria can easily grow in a woman's cervix, uterus, and fallopian tubes. They can also grow in a man's urethra, which is the urine canal. When a person has sex with another person who has gonorrhea, these bacteria are passed from one person to another.

The bacteria can be passed from one person to another through vaginal, oral, and anal sex. Bacteria living in a man's urethra can be transferred to a woman's vagina during sex, and they can also be transferred to a person's anus during anal sex. It is also possible to catch an STD through oral sex, as the bacteria living in a man's or woman's genitals can be transferred to a person's mouth. A sexually transmitted virus can also be spread this way. Although some people consider oral and anal sex to be safe ways to have sex, this is not true. STDs can easily be spread through any kind of sexual contact. "All sex is sex and is a way you can acquire sexually transmitted diseases," noted Stuart

Berman. "The infection is a bit different, the implications are a bit different, but lots of kids are appalled to learn they can get gonorrhea of the throat, and they can get syphilis orally."[62]

Syphilis is another STD that is caused by bacteria. This disease is highly infectious, and a person gets it by coming into direct contact with a syphilis sore. These sores are generally on the outside of a person's genitals, in the anus, in the rectum, or in a woman's vagina, but they can also be found on the lips and mouth. When a cut or the mucous membrane of the vagina or anus comes into contact with the syphilis sore, a person becomes infected with syphilis.

Infections with No Cure

Other STDs are caused by viruses. These microscopic organisms live and reproduce inside host cells. An STD caused by a virus can be treated but not cured.

One STD caused by a virus is herpes. The herpes simplex virus is the cause of cold sores as well as genital herpes.

HSV-1 is typically associated with cold sores. The majority of people come into contact with this common and highly contagious virus as children, through kisses from friends or relatives. Around 90 percent of Americans have been exposed to HSV-1. The virus typically causes redness, bumps, or blisters on the lips or inside the mouth that heal within a few days.

Most cases of genital herpes are caused by HSV-2. A person can get genital herpes through sexual contact with someone who is infected with the virus. Although the majority of genital herpes is caused by HSV-2, it is possible for HSV-1 to also cause genital herpes. A person who has HSV-1 in the mouth can infect a person's genitals through oral sex. People can also get HSV-1 or HSV-2 through sexual intercourse. There are antiviral drugs that can be used to treat genital herpes that make the outbreaks less severe.

Another STD caused by a virus is AIDS, which is caused by HIV. HIV is most commonly passed from one person to another through sex or by sharing needles or syringes with a person who injects drugs and has HIV. The virus can also be passed from a mother to her baby before the baby is born, during birth, or when the baby is breastfed after birth. The difference between HIV and other viruses is that it attacks the body's immune system, destroying a type of white blood cell the body needs to fight disease. People with the virus can be treated with anti-HIV medications to keep them healthy.

A third STD-causing virus is the human papillomavirus (HPV), which is most commonly spread through vaginal or anal intercourse. There are more than 40 subtypes of HPV that infect the genital area. Although the body sometimes naturally fights off the virus, some of these subtypes may cause a person to develop genital warts or cervical cancer. These subtypes bring on different symptoms and require their own treatments.

Bacterial Vaginosis

A very common STD in women is called bacterial vaginosis (BV). Doctors are not sure what causes it, but the infection typically occurs in sexually active women. BV is caused when there is an imbalance of "good" and "bad" bacteria found in a woman's vagina. The good bacteria (lactobacilli) should outnumber the bad (anaerobes). Having a new sex partner or multiple partners can upset this balance. BV infections are more common in women who have sex with women. Symptoms of BV include vaginal itching or burning during urination and a foul-smelling, whitish discharge. Treatment includes either oral antibiotics or vaginal creams. Not treating BV can lead to other STDs, such as PID, and premature labor for pregnant women.

Protect Yourself

Some may think that the best way to keep these infectious bacteria and viruses from getting into their body is abstinence. However, that depends on the definition of abstinence. True abstinence means not engaging in any sexual activity with someone else, which would eliminate the risk of getting an STD. Some people engage in selective abstinence, which means they participate in some sexual activities but not intercourse. These activities still could put the person at risk for some STDs if certain precautions are not taken.

Being in a long-term, monogamous relationship with one person who has been tested and is known not to be infected is another way to avoid getting an STD. Being faithful to a partner and having a partner who is also faithful is critical. If people are having sex while in a relationship, it is important to remember that they are protected against STDs only if each person in the relationship does not have sex with others. "If you're free of infection yourself, your risk also is zero if you have sex only with one *uninfected* partner," noted researcher Charles Ebel. "As soon as either partner has a new sexual contact, however, all bets are off."[63]

If you are having sex, using a condom will reduce your chances of getting an STD. A condom is a covering of latex or plastic that unrolls onto the penis. To increase the chances that it will prevent a person from getting an STD, it should be placed onto the erect penis before genital contact, and it should be removed at the end of intercourse. There is also a female condom, which is a polyurethane or latex sheath that lines the vagina. It is inserted into the vagina like a tampon. Dental dams are another barrier method in STD prevention. It is a thin, square piece of rubber placed over the vagina for female oral sex.

Partners who have been tested for STDs and are in a monogamous relationship are at a lower risk of getting an STD.

Using a condom is not a 100 percent guarantee that a person will not get an STD, but it is a person's best protection. There are different types of condoms, and some provide more protection than others. The most reliable condoms are standard latex condoms, which are about 98 percent effective. Non-latex condoms are also available, but the World Health Organization (WHO) reports that they have a higher rate of breakage, reducing their efficiency to 95 percent. Lambskin condoms do not protect against all STDs because the natural pores in lambskin are large enough to let viruses such as HIV or herpes through. When female condoms are inserted correctly, they are about 95 percent effective in preventing STDs.

Condoms have other limitations as well. They offer good protection against getting a bacterial STD such as gonorrhea or chlamydia. However, a condom is not as good at offering complete protection against an STD that is spread through a sore or lesion on the skin because it might not cover the area that can cause an STD infection. For example, a condom only protects against syphilis when the infected area or the site of potential exposure is protected or covered. Syphilis sores can occur in areas that are not covered by a condom. HPV can also be present throughout a person's genital area, not only in the place covered by a condom. The herpes virus is another STD that can be spread from one person to another even though a condom is used, as the area shedding the virus may not be covered. Despite its limitations, however, a condom remains the best line of defense against STDs.

To increase their effectiveness, condoms need to be used both consistently and correctly. According to the CDC, this means using a new condom every time. The CDC has specific guidelines for putting the condom on and removal and disposal without coming into contact with bodily fluids. The CDC also recommends using condoms with water-based lubricants, because oil-based lubricants such as petroleum jelly or massage oils can weaken condoms and cause them to break. Condoms should not be stored in a wallet or other warm place, and the package should be checked for an expiration date.

In preventing HIV, using a condom makes sex 10,000 times safer than when a condom is not used.

The Young and the Reckless

There are a few reasons why STDs are so rampant among young people. Young people may underestimate the risk of getting an STD or think that it is not a big deal to have one because treatments are available, as Anthony L. Contreras said. They do not understand how having an STD could change their life. He has said the hardest thing about dealing with young people and STDs is "trying to make them see there still is risk involved."[64]

According to a study published in the *Journal of Adolescent Health* in 2016, although they make up nearly half of new STD cases each year, most young people do not even get tested for STDs. For many, this was due to a lack of understanding of the risks. Other teens worried about the cost of the testing. Another concern was confidentiality. As of 2016, young people can stay on their parents' health care plans until they are 26, but there is nothing stopping insurers from sending notices to the policyholders, the parents, of testing or services that were provided. According to Abigail English, Director of the Center for Adolescent Health and the Law, young adults over 18 "have the same privacy rights as other adults, but their situation is complicated because they're on a plan with someone else who is the policyholder."[65]

Sometimes it takes getting an STD to make a teen realize that he or she is no different from anyone else and has as much chance as anyone of getting an STD. The feeling of invulnerability persists until the teen faces the consequences of his or her behavior.

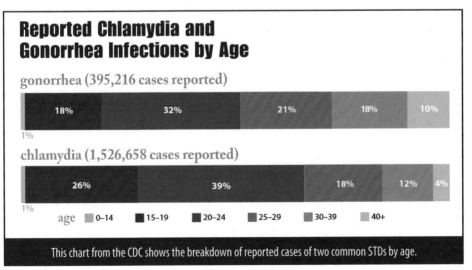

Reported Chlamydia and Gonorrhea Infections by Age

gonorrhea (395,216 cases reported)

| 18% | 32% | 21% | 18% | 10% |

1%

chlamydia (1,526,658 cases reported)

| 26% | 39% | 18% | 12% | 4% |

1%

age ▪ 0–14 ▪ 15–19 ▪ 20–24 ▪ 25–29 ▪ 30–39 ▪ 40+

This chart from the CDC shows the breakdown of reported cases of two common STDs by age.

Blame the Media

It is easy to be lulled into thinking that sex has no consequences by the images of sex portrayed on television and elsewhere in the media. The characters on television shows aimed at teens are rarely shown using condoms or dealing with gonorrhea or herpes. Ross O'Hara, a post-doctoral fellow at the University of Missouri conducted research into sexual behavior in popular movies and how it affects adolescent sexual behavior. The six-year study showed that "adolescents who are exposed to more sexual content in movies start having sex at younger ages, have more sexual partners, and are less likely to use condoms with casual sexual partners,"[66] O'Hara said.

A study by the journal *Pediatrics* found that white teens with the highest level of exposure to sexual content in the media were 120 percent more likely to have initiated sexual intercourse.

O'Hara and his colleagues focused on sensation-seeking behavior, which during adolescence, is almost natural because of the peaks of hormone changes. They found that more exposure to sexual content led to an increase of sensation-seeking behaviors that sometimes lasted until a person was in their 20s. "These movies appear to fundamentally influence their personality through changes in sensation-seeking," O'Hara said, "Which has far-reaching implications for all of their risk-taking behaviors."[67]

Researchers also believe that adolescents use movies as sexual scripts and use them as examples of how to behave in these situations in real life. In fact, 57 percent of young people between the ages of 14 and 16 get most of their sexual information from the screen. Most recent films barely mention contraception at all.

Silent Diseases

Another reason that STDs continue to spread is because many people do not realize they have them and do not seek treatment. They may pass an STD on to another person without even realizing they are infected with one. An STD often shows no symptoms, and unless a person is tested, it is impossible to tell if he or she has the disease. "Most of the infections people get don't cause symptoms," Berman noted. "And the fact that you don't have any overt symptoms, or your partner has no symptoms, should be no reassurance. The great majority of STDs are probably transferred by people who have no symptoms and didn't know they had it."[68]

Open Communication

Having open, honest communication with your doctor is crucial when dealing with STDs. Doctors

How to Tell a Partner about an STD

Ella Dawson, who is open about her herpes diagnosis, gave a few pointers on telling a sexual partner about an STD. Here are a few from her article posted at womenshealthmag.com:

- Practice saying, "I have an STD" in front of the mirror.

- Make it a conversation; give your partner time to talk and express his or her feelings.

- Offer information about the disease, but do not give too much information. You should not feel like you have to share how you got it.

- Do not apologize—you have nothing to be ashamed of, and coming across as confident will put your partner at ease.

- Give your partner time to think. They may need space or time to do research.

- Do not wait—you must tell your partner before you have sex for the first time, otherwise you will have something to apologize for.

Even though telling a partner about an STD may be difficult, it could build more trust in the relationship and make it even better.

are nonjudgmental when it comes to treating their patients and their only concern is to cure the disease or help make it more manageable. In most states, after a young person turns 13, they can get a confidential test and parents do not need to be notified of a positive STD test. Planned Parenthood is a great resource for teens who need confidential testing and information about birth control. If a teen does want to confide in a parent, health care professionals can help bring up the subject and help parents understand the treatment the teen needs. Sometimes parents can surprise their teen and not be as judgmental as they might think.

The topic of STDs can be a tough subject to discuss with parents, and it can be even more difficult to talk about with a boyfriend or girlfriend. It is not easy, but teens should bring up the issues of protection and STD testing with any potential sex partners. A person may not be thinking about STDs in the heat of the moment, but the danger is still there. Although the topic may not be easy to talk about, it is not pleasant to live with the consequences of an STD, either. Being mature enough to have sex means being responsible enough to take precautions and to bring up the topic of STDs.

CHAPTER FIVE

REVERSING THE TREND

The rising trend in STD infections has signaled to the world of health care that things need to change. Budget cuts to STD care and prevention programs are one of the biggest problems. According to David Harvey, executive director for the National Coalition of STD Directors, "We believe there's a direct relationship between budget cuts and increases in STDs in the United States. There has been no federal increases for STD programs in this country since 2003."[69]

The way to combat this is to put money back into the programs that have worked so well in the past. Dr. Gail Bolan recommends the tracking systems that collect data on new cases be improved, and that people need to have more access to clinics for treatment. "We have reached a decisive moment for the nation," according to Dr. Jonathan Mermin. "STD rates are rising, and many of the country's systems for preventing STDs have eroded," he said. "We must mobilize, rebuild and expand services—or the human and economic burden will continue to grow."[70]

Taking Action

Organizations such as the Centers for Disease Control and Prevention are working to prevent people from getting STDs. The organization views the prevention of STDs as one way of keeping people healthy, and it is spreading its message about the dangers of STDs to people through health departments in large cities, as well as through community groups. In the CDC's 2015 report, the "National Overview of Sexually Transmitted Diseases," it was stated, "All Americans should have the opportunity to make choices that lead to health and wellness. Working together, interested, committed public and private organizations, communities, and individuals can take action to prevent sexually transmitted diseases (STDs) and their related health consequences."[71]

The CDC has combined print, video, and online materials to share information about HIV. The CDC's Division of Adolescent and School Health (DASH) gives support for STD prevention in the nation's public schools. DASH supports the development of STD educational programs for middle school students and their parents, creates educational tools to implement the programs, and conducts ongoing research to measure their effectiveness. The CDC's Act Against AIDS program launched a campaign called #DoingIt designed to motivate everyone to get regular HIV testing. Act Against AIDS is also promoting HIV awareness in the Latinx community, who account for 23 percent of new HIV infections each year.

Peer education has proven to be effective in spreading the word about STDs. Studies have shown that when STD prevention comes from their peers, adolescents are more likely to openly participate in discussions and recognize the personal dangers of STDs. A study of one clinic showed that contraceptive use increased 40 percent among teens who were counseled by their peers.

Online campaigns are also a great way to reach out to people. Iwannaknow.org, sponsored by the American Sexual Health Association, has resources and information for teens to direct them on where to get testing and treatment. HIV Equal was started in 2013 and is led by *Project Runway* contestant Jack Mackenroth, who is HIV positive. HIV Equal encourages people to post photos of themselves getting an HIV test on social media. Eventually, Mackenroth wants to set up mobile testing sites and photo shoots all over the country. The STD Project provides community support for people diagnosed with STDs through an anonymous forum where they can share their stories.

One study found that 30 percent of new HIV infections were transmitted by someone who did not know they had the disease. Testing is the first step in protecting and prolonging one's life.

Get Tested Early and Often

Regular testing and early treatment is essential in stopping the spread of STDs. Antibiotics easily treat the early stages of chlamydia, gonorrhea, and syphilis. Treating these STDs also controls the spread of HIV because a person who has an STD is more susceptible to contracting HIV. Antiviral medications can help reduce the severity of a genital herpes outbreak and lessen the chance for future outbreaks.

Antiretroviral therapy drugs are the standard treatment for people with HIV. It involves taking several drugs, sometimes called a drug "cocktail." These medicines prevent the HIV virus from multiplying, giving the immune system a chance to recover from fighting off infections. Reducing the amount of HIV in the body also lessens the possibility for the infected person to transmit the disease to someone else. When to start the drug cocktail is still under debate. Some doctors believe in prescribing it right away, and others think that it is best to put off taking the cocktail for as long as possible because of harmful side effects and possible drug resistance.

Be Suspicious of Home Treatments

The only way to diagnose and treat STDs is by going to a doctor and following their prescribed medications exactly as instructed. While the Internet may be a useful tool for information, be suspicious of home remedies that claim they can cure or treat an STD. One of these pseudoscientific studies was on mouthwash and gonorrhea of the throat or mouth.

A clinical trial involved a small group of gay and bisexual men who had tested positive for gonorrhea of the throat or mouth. Some were given Listerine to gargle with, and the rest of the men gargled with a saline solution. The men gargling with Listerine were 80 percent less likely to test positive for gonorrhea after 5 minutes than the saline group. However, no further testing has been done with this theory. Possibly, the ingredients in the Listerine threw off the test results and created a false negative or it only reduces bacteria levels for the short term. Regardless, the best policy is always for a person to protect themselves and their partner and see a doctor for an approved medication and testing.

Getting Him to the Doctor

Men who show no symptoms of having an STD can be especially reluctant to take the time to seek treatment and pay for a visit to a doctor. "The real problem is getting the guys treated,"[72] Suzanne Swanson said.

One reason for this is that there are no federal recommendations for men to get tested annually. While it is true that the health problems for women with STDs are much more serious, the U.S. Preventive Services Task Force says that if men are not screened, STD rates in women will remain the same. Also, men seek health care services less frequently than women in general. Other issues for men include not having insurance and not knowing where to go. Many are too embarrassed to go to a clinic.

In Los Angeles, California, where the STD rates are among the highest in the country, county programs invested in mobile units where people could get free testing. A study by the Washington University School of

Medicine revealed that men who were able to test at home with a free STD kit were 60 percent more likely to get tested than those who had to go to a clinic. Dr. Bradley Stoner, associate professor at Washington University, said, "After you get out of high school in United States, men might not see the doctor till they get older and have [a] health problem, and I think that is one of the problems, identifying opportunities for doing male screenings."[73]

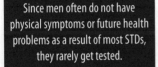

Since men often do not have physical symptoms or future health problems as a result of most STDs, they rarely get tested.

Researchers are always looking for more efficient and effective ways to test and treat STDs. The Gardasil vaccine, released in 2006, protects young women against vaginal, cervical, anal, and vulvar cancers, as well as genital warts, that are caused by nine subtypes of HPV. The vaccine is also recommended for young men and protects against genital warts and anal cancers caused by these same HPV subtypes. The vaccine is recommended for people aged 9 to 26. People 9 through 14 years old should receive 2 or 3 doses of the HPV vaccine, with the second shot being given between 6 and 12 months after the first shot. Teens and young adults who start the series between the ages of 15 and 26 will need three doses of the vaccine, with the second dose occurring two months after the first and the third shot occurring six months after the first.

Other prevention efforts include research work on other vaccines and topical microbicides, which would be used to prevent STD infection in different ways. Topical microbicides that would prevent STDs would be applied before sexual intercourse and are in the form of a gel or cream. The topical microbicides would not offer long-term protection and would need to be reapplied.

So far, research has produced mixed results with STD vaccines. Scientists have not yet been able to develop a vaccine that offers protection against herpes. However, recent studies have shown some breakthroughs in the development of an HIV vaccine. In 2012, researchers were encouraged when a vaccine study in Thailand exposed vulnerability in the HIV virus. Those results led researchers to develop another HIV vaccine, and in 2016, a research study on the new vaccine was started in South Africa, where more than 7 million people are infected with the virus. Although these trials have a long history of failures because of the resiliency of the virus, researchers are optimistic. According to Anthony Fauci, director of the National Institute of Allergy and Infectious Diseases, this experiment "is taking the only modestly successful vaccine trial ... and trying to improve upon it in a higher-risk population."[74] Thembi Dlamini, a 29-year-old South African woman and participant in the trial, guesses that about half of her friends are HIV positive, and her sister passed away from AIDS 5 years earlier. "I don't want to lose another member of my family," Thembi Dlamini said. "I want to be one of the ones who helped prevent this thing for the future."[75]

Shown here is an African woman being tested for HIV. Africa has the most serious HIV epidemic in the world.

The Virginity Pledge

Teens who sign a virginity pledge and vow to abstain from sex before marriage often break that pledge, a study indicates. A 2008 study published in *Pediatrics* by Janet Rosenbaum indicates that teens who signed a virginity pledge were just as likely to have taken part in sexual behavior as teens who did not sign a pledge. They were also less likely to use condoms to protect themselves against STDs or use birth control than teens who had not signed a pledge.

The U.S. government spent more than $2 billion in funding for abstinence-only programs between 1997 and 2017. These do not allow education on birth control or safe sex. Rosenbaum believes that these abstinence-only sexual education programs should be replaced by programs that teach young people about safe sex. She supports evidence-based sexual education programs and believes funding should go toward those programs instead, especially because abstinence-only programs have been shown to have little impact on the number of teens having sex.

According to studies that have been conducted, teens who take a virginity pledge are just as likely to take part in sexual behavior as teens who do not.

Keep the Conversation Going

Every year, millions of dollars are poured into the research and treatment of STDs, yet STD rates keep increasing. Information about STDs and how to prevent them is more accessible to the general public than it ever was. So where is the breakdown? With federal funds evaporating and clinics closing all over the country, it is up to society to keep the conversation about STDs going, no matter how uncomfortable or embarrassing it may be.

Being able to talk to a partner about contraception is essential. If a person cannot have a conversation with their partner about safe sex, then they are not ready to have sex at all. Not only should they talk about safe sex and STDs, they should also be able to talk honestly about the relationship and whether it is monogamous or not. If someone is uncomfortable participating in sexual activity, they must be able to say "no" without worrying about ruining their relationship.

Being honest with a health care provider is also important. Their job is not to judge, but to treat and prevent the spread of STDs. Without open communication, the stigma about STDs will continue.

It is important to keep the conversation about STDs going in an attempt to prevent the rate of people getting them from rising.

Finding out about an STD diagnosis is traumatic. There is anger, embarrassment, shame, and maybe betrayal by a loved one. There is the fear of getting sick and getting others sick. Some STDs will change a person's life forever. Luckily, today there are dozens of organizations easily available to anyone who needs them, and there are health care professionals and scientists dedicated to halting this rising trend and turning it around. According to Dr. Gail Bolan, "Life can be complicated, but good sexual health doesn't have to be. Just remember these three things to protect yourself— *Talk. Test. Treat.*"[76]

Dr. Gail Bolan received the CDC's Jack Spencer award in 2010 for her career accomplishments in STD prevention.

Introduction: It Can Happen to Anyone

1. Susan Cohen, telephone interview by author of *Sexually Transmitted Diseases*, April 24, 2009.

2. Amber, "My Name Is Amber," The Naked Truth, 2016. www.nakedtruth.idaho.gov/amber.aspx.

3. Amber, "My Name Is Amber."

4. Stuart Berman, telephone interview by author of *Sexually Transmitted Diseases*, May 1, 2009.

Chapter One: A Worsening Epidemic

5. Jenelle Marie Pierce, "The STD Project," Accessed April 27, 2017. www.thestdproject.com/std-interviews-share-your-story.

6. "2015 STD Surveillance Report Press Release," Centers for Disease Control and Prevention, October 19, 2016. www.cdc.gov/nchhstp/newsroom/2016/std-surveillance-report-2015-press-release.html.

7. Berman, interview.

8. Suzanne Swanson, telephone interview by author of *Sexually Transmitted Diseases*, April 14, 2009.

9. "Cervical Cancer—General Information," Marshall University, accessed May 3, 2017. www.marshall.edu/wcenter/breast-and-cervical-cancer/cervical-cancer-general-information/.

10. Dr. Jill Grimes, telephone interview by author of *Sexually Transmitted Diseases*, April 14, 2009.

11. Richard, "I was Just 20," The Naked Truth, 2016. www.nakedtruth.idaho.gov/richard.aspx.

12. Anthony L. Contreras, telephone interview by author of *Sexually Transmitted Diseases*, April 17, 2009.

13. Grimes, interview.

14. Maria, telephone interview by author of *Sexually Transmitted Diseases*, April 12, 2009.

15. "I Suffer from a Stigma, not a Disease: Personal Stories," American Sexual Health Association (ASHA), 2017. www.ashasexualhealth.org/sexual-health/personal-stories.

16. Cohen, interview.

Chapter Two: Screening and Diagnosis

17. "The Naked Truth," www.nakedtruth.idaho.gov/sara.aspx.

18. "The Naked Truth."

19. Lisa Marr, *Sexually Transmitted Diseases: A Physician Tells You What You Need to Know.* Baltimore, MD: Johns Hopkins University Press, 1998, p. 28.

20. Marr, Sexually Transmitted Diseases, p. 36.

21. Marr, Sexually Transmitted Diseases, p. 291.

22. Berman, interview.

Chapter Three: After the Diagnosis

23. "Chlamydia- It's Opened My Eyes- STD Interviews," The STD Project. www.thestdproject.com/chlamydia-its-opened-my-eyes-std-interviews.

24. "Chlamydia- It's Opened My Eyes- STD Interviews."

25. Jenelle Marie Pierce, "If I Could, Would I Go Back in Time and Change my Genital Herpes?," Better2Know. www.better2know.co.uk/blog/if-i-could-would-i-go-back-in-time-and-change-my-genital-herpes.

26. Maria, interview.

27. Maria, interview.

28. Maria, interview.

29. Maria, interview.

30. Maria, interview.

31. Maria, interview.

32. Maria, interview.

33. Maria, interview.

34. Kelly, telephone interview by author of *Sexually Transmitted Diseases*, April 2009.

35. Kelly, interview.

36. Kelly, interview.

37. Kelly, interview.

38. Kelly, interview.

39. Kelly, interview.

40. Kelly, interview.

41. Michelle, telephone interview by author of *Sexually Transmitted Diseases*, April 2009.

42. Michelle, interview.

43. Michelle, interview.

44. Michelle, interview.

45. Michelle, interview.

46. Michelle, interview.

47. Michelle, interview.

48. Contreras, interview.

49. Contreras, interview.

50. Contreras, interview.

51. Contreras, interview.

52. Contreras, interview.

53. Contreras, interview.

54. Contreras, interview.

55. Contreras, interview.

56. Contreras, interview.

57. Tom, telephone interview by author of *Sexually Transmitted Diseases*, June 11, 2009.

58. Tom, interview.

59. Tom, interview.

Chapter Four: Stopping the Spread of STDs

60. "I Knew it was a Risk for my Health But…: Personal Stories," American Sexual Health Association (ASHA), 2017. www.ashasexualhealth.org/sexual-health/personal-stories.

61. Cohen, interview.

62. Berman, interview.

63. Charles Ebel, *Managing Herpes: How to Live and Love with a Chronic STD*. Triangle Park, NC: American Social Health Association, 1998, p. 209.

64. Contreras, interview.

65. Michelle Andrews, "Young People At Risk For STDs Often Don't Get Tested: Study," Kaiser Health News, June 3, 2016. khn.org/news/young-people-at-risk-for-stds-often-dont-get-tested-study.

66. "Exposure to Sexual Content in Popular Movies Predicts Sexual Behavior in Adolescence," Association for Psychological Science, July 17, 2012. www.psychologicalscience.org/news/releases/exposure-to-sexual-content-in-popular-movies-predicts-sexual-behavior-in-adolescence.html#.WHkXmLksrkd.

67. "Exposure to Sexual Content in Popular Movies Predicts Sexual Behavior in Adolescence."

68. Berman, interview.

Chapter Five: Reversing the Trend

69. Angus Chen, "STD Infections Rise To New Highs After States Close Health Clinics," NPR, October 20, 2016. www.npr.org/sections/health-shots/2016/10/20/498719092/std-infections-rise-to-new-highs-after-states-close-health-clinics.

70. Jacqueline Howard, "STD Rates Reach Record High in United States," CNN, October 20, 2016. www.cnn.com/2016/10/20/health/std-statistics-record-high.

71. "National Overview of Sexually Transmitted Diseases (STDs)," Centers for Disease Control and Prevention, 2015. www.cdc.gov/std/stats15/natoverview.htm.

72. Swanson, interview.

73. Signe Okkels Larsen, "Why Men Don't Get Tested for STDs," Annenburg Media Center, University of Southern California, November 5, 2014. www.neontommy.com/news/2014/10/why-men-dont-get-tested-stds.

74. Quoted in Ryan Lenora Brown and Lenny Bernstein, "Major HIV Vaccine Trial

in South Africa Stokes Hope," *The Washington Post*, November 25, 2016. www. washingtonpost.com/national/health-science/ major-hiv-vaccine-trial-in-south-africa-again-stokes-hope/2016/11/25/188cd56a-b0ff-11e6-be1c-8cec35b1ad25_story.html?utm_term=.5e8f18f4f406.

75. Quoted in Ryan Lenora Brown and Lenny Berstein, "Major HIV Vaccine Trial in South Africa Stokes Hope."

76. Dr. Gail Bolan, "STD Awareness Month: CDC Encourages Everyone to Talk, Test, and Treat," AIDS.gov, April 20, 2016. blog.aids. gov/2016/04/std-awareness-month-cdc-encourages-everyone-to-talk-test-and-treat.html.

abstinence: The choice not to have sex.

acquired immunodeficiency syndrome (AIDS): A life-threatening condition caused by the human immunodeficiency virus (HIV). HIV damages the immune system, making a person susceptible to some infections and cancers.

bacteria: Single-celled organisms visible only under a microscope. Some bacteria cause infection, but others are beneficial.

cervix: The narrow outer end of the uterus.

chlamydia: A common STD caused by bacteria. It spreads easily and is curable.

condom: A thin covering made of latex or polyurethane that fits over the penis.

ectopic pregnancy: A pregnancy in which the fertilized egg implants in a woman's fallopian tube rather than in the uterus.

fallopian tubes: The part of a woman's reproductive system that transports the egg from the ovary to the uterus.

genital herpes: An STD caused by a virus that causes blisters, generally in the genital area.

genitals: A person's sex organs.

gonorrhea: A common STD that is caused by bacteria.

herpes simplex virus: A viral infection mainly affecting the mouth or genital area. Herpes simplex virus type 1 (HSV-1) is generally associated with an infection of the mouth. Herpes simplex virus type 2 (HSV-2) is typically associated with genital sores.

human immunodeficiency virus (HIV): The virus that causes acquired immunodeficiency syndrome (AIDS).

human papillomavirus (HPV): A virus with many subtypes that may cause genital warts or cervical cancer.

lesion: A change in the structure of a body part due to injury or disease.

stigma: A mark of shame.

syphilis: An STD caused by bacteria. It progresses through several stages and, if left untreated, can lead to blindness, mental problems, and death.

uterus: An organ in a woman's reproductive system where the fetus grows; it is also called the womb.

virus: A microscopic organism that lives and reproduces inside host cells and is the cause of some infectious diseases.

American Sexual Health Association (ASHA)
PO Box 13827
Research Triangle Park, NC 27709
(919) 361-8400
info@ashasexualhealth.org
www.ashasexualhealth.org/
The ASHA offers accurate and reliable information about sexually transmitted infections. This nonprofit organization, founded in 1914, works to improve public health as it focuses on STDs. Its publications include patient educational materials, such as a quarterly newsletter about herpes treatment and research, as well as pamphlets, books, and fact sheets on a variety of topics relating to STDs.

Centers for Disease Control and Prevention (CDC)
1600 Clifton Rd.
Atlanta, GA 30329
(800) 232-4636
www.cdc.gov
The CDC is the top public health agency in the United States. As part of the U.S. Department of Health and Human Services, it focuses on the prevention and control of disease, injury, and disability to protect people's health and promote quality of life. It responds to health threats and offers information on a wide variety of diseases and health-related topics. Information and brochures about specific STDs can be found on its website.

National Institute of Allergy and Infectious Diseases
5601 Fishers Lane, MSC 9806
Bethesda, MD 20892
(866) 284-4107
www.niaid.nih.gov
This organization conducts and supports research into infectious diseases as well as allergic diseases. It is part of the U.S. Department of Health and Human Services and the National Institutes of Health. Its research has led to new treatments, vaccines, and tests. It publishes free pamphlets about topics including the immune system and vaccines, as well as fact sheets about chlamydia, genital herpes, gonorrhea, and other STDs.

Office on Women's Health
Department of Health and Human Services
200 Independence Avenue, SW Room 712E
Washington, DC 20201
(800) 994-9662
www.womenshealth.gov
Part of the U.S. Department of Health and Human Services, this organization advocates the health and well-being of women. It promotes health equity for women and girls through programs, education of health professionals, and health information for consumers. Its free publications answer frequently asked questions about STDs and other health concerns.

Planned Parenthood Federation of America
123 William Street, 10th floor
New York, NY 10038
(800) 230-7526
www.plannedparenthood.org
This organization offers information on sexual and reproductive health care. It operates more than 650 health centers nationwide and offers testing and treatment for STDs. It also provides sex education, offering information about STD prevention.

FOR MORE INFORMATION

Books

Collins, Nicholas, and Samuel G. Woods. *Frequently Asked Questions about STDs*. New York, NY: Rosen Publishing, 2012.
This book answers the big questions about STDs that teens may be afraid to ask.

Forna, Fatu. *From Your Doctor To You: What Every Teenage Girl Should Know About Her Body, Sex, STDs and Contraception*. Colorado Springs, CO: CreateSpace Independent Publishing Platform, 2014.
This book, written by a gynecologist, answers many uncomfortable questions for girls about sex and STDs.

Grimes, Jill. *Seductive Delusions: How Everyday People Catch STIs*. Baltimore, MD: Johns Hopkins University Press, 2016.
Grimes delivers the facts on STDs by looking at them through the eyes of people infected with them.

Overton, Sheila, and Treacy Colbert. *Before It's Too Late: A Parent's Guide on Teens, Sex, and Sanity*. Bloomington, IN: iUniverse, 2016.
This is a guide for both teens and parents to help teens make smart decisions about sexual behavior.

Warren, Terri. *The Good News About the Bad News: Herpes: Everything You Need to Know*. Oakland, CA: New Harbinger Publications, 2009.
This book is a complete guide to living with genital herpes and its stigma.

Websites

Eunice Kennedy Shriver National Institute of Child Health and Human Development
www.nichd.nih.gov/health/topics/stds/Pages/default.aspx
This website, run by the National Institutes of Health, includes information on STDs, including research and clinical trials.

MedlinePlus
medlineplus.gov/sexuallytransmitteddiseases.html
This website, run by the U.S. National Library of Medicine, has detailed information on STDs, pregnancy, and condoms.

National Prevention Information Network
npin.cdc.gov/pages/contact-us
NPIN distributes information about STDs and other diseases. In addition to producing materials, it also catalogs and collects information that can be shared and used by people working in fields related to those diseases.

TeensHealth
kidshealth.org/en/teens/std.html
TeensHealth has plenty of articles on STDs, birth control, and talking to a partner about STDs.

Teen Source
www.teensource.org/std
This website provides information on STDs, including how they can be contracted and treated, and also has information on birth control and a map to find a clinic in a certain area.

Cover kadmy/iStock/Thinkstock; cover, pp. 2–3, 4–5, 6–7, 10, 13, 21, 25, 34, 37, 42, 49, 52, 56, 59, 64, 72, 74, 77, 82, 85, 91, 93, 95, 97, 103, 104 (purple texture) foxaon1987/ Shutterstock.com; p. 8 karelnoppe/Shutterstock.com; p. 11 Katherine Welles/Shutterstock.com; p. 15 Mehau Kulyk/ Science Photo Library/Getty Images; pp. 17, 35 Alexander Raths/Shutterstock.com; p. 19 italay/Shutterstock.com; pp. 22, 69, 84 courtesy of CDC.gov; p. 26 Monkey Business Images/Shutterstock.com; p. 29 Jochen Schoenfeld/ Shutterstock.com; p. 32 TisforThan/Shutterstock.com; p. 37 Kateryna Kon/Shutterstock.com; p. 39 Science Picture Co/Collection Mix: Subjects/Getty Images; p. 45 tommaso79/iStock/Thinkstock; p. 49 Marian Wilson/Shutterstock.com; p. 52 Komsan Loonprom/ Shutterstock.com; p. 55 Hero Images/Getty Images; pp. 60–61 Africa Studio/Shutterstock.com; p. 66 Dean Drobot/Shutterstock.com; p. 68 domnitsky/ Shutterstock.com; p. 70 Goncharov_Artem/ Shutterstock.com; p. 72 hoozone/E+/Getty Images; p. 76 Room's Studio/Shutterstock.com; pp. 78–79 AndreyPopov/iStock/Thinkstock; p. 81 Gianluigi Guercia/ AFP/Getty Images; p. 82 Marvi Lacar/Getty Images; p. 83 © istockphoto.com/sturti.

Christine Honders lives in Upstate New York with her husband and her three children. She has written more than 25 books for young people and considers sexual health to be a primary concern among adolescents.

31901060924091